Coaching
Mentoring

Florence Stone

- Fast track route to coaching and mentoring top performers for individual and organizational success

- Covers the key areas of coaching and mentoring, from conducting a training needs assessment and reinforcing quality performance and employee accountability to empowering top performers and applying mentoring to succession planning and diversity management

- Examples and lessons from some of the world's most successful organizations, including Saturn, Arthur Andersen, General Electric, Johnson & Johnson, Royal Dutch Shell, the World Bank and Analog Devices Inc, and ideas from the smartest thinkers, including Abraham Maslow, Frederick Herzberg, Douglas McGregor, Peter Drucker and Jack Welch

- Includes a glossary of key concepts and a comprehensive resources guide

LEADING

08.09

≫EXPRESS EXEC. COM≪
essential management thinking at your fingertips

First published 2002 by
Capstone Publishing (a Wiley company)
8 Newtec Place
Magdalen Road
Oxford OX4 1RE
United Kingdom
http://www.capstoneideas.com

CIP catalogue records for this book are available from the British Library and the US Library of Congress

ISBN 1-84112-208-4

Printed and bound in Great Britain

This book is printed on acid-free paper

Substantial discounts on bulk quantities of Capstone books are available to corporations, professional associations and other organizations. Please contact Capstone for more details on +44 (0)1865 798 623 or (fax) +44 (0)1865 240 941 or (e-mail) info@wiley-capstone.co.uk

Contents

Introduction to ExpressExec

ExpressExec is 3 million words of the latest management thinking compiled into 10 modules. Each module contains 10 individual titles forming a comprehensive resource of current business practice written by leading practitioners in their field. From brand management to balanced scorecard, ExpressExec enables you to grasp the key concepts behind each subject and implement the theory immediately. Each of the 100 titles is available in print and electronic formats.

Through the ExpressExec.com Website you will discover that you can access the complete resource in a number of ways:

» printed books or e-books;
» e-content – PDF or XML (for licensed syndication) adding value to an intranet or Internet site;
» a corporate e-learning/knowledge management solution providing a cost-effective platform for developing skills and sharing knowledge within an organization;
» bespoke delivery – tailored solutions to solve your need.

Why not visit www.expressexec.com and register for free key management briefings, a monthly newsletter and interactive skills checklists. Share your ideas about ExpressExec and your thoughts about business today.

Please contact elound@wiley-capstone.co.uk for more information.

Introduction

Discover:

» how coaching can improve job skills and thereby performance;
» how mentoring is as important to job performance as career advancement; and
» how coaching and mentoring is different from counseling.

The business environment has changed dramatically. High performance is no longer an option, whether the organization competes only regionally or in the international marketplace. Technological changes bring new challenges daily. But they are not the sole source of the increased pressure within organizations.

Right now, we are experiencing worldwide a decline in the economy, the depth of downturn different from country to country but very much a reality, if not a fear.

If your organization is to sustain its competitive advantage, it needs employees who are productive and willing to continually learn and adapt as their roles change along with the organization. Today's companies need people who at best exceed expectations and at worst meet standards. Managers with good people skills can get that kind of performance from their employees from coaching and mentoring.

This book will help you to:

» understand the coaching and mentoring processes;
» overcome pitfalls and maximize the benefits of these performance management tools;
» learn how to incorporate one or both programs into your own company's best practices.

Coaching is the process by which employees gain the skills, abilities, and knowledge they need to develop themselves professionally and become more effective in their jobs. When you coach your employees, you increase both their performance in their current jobs and their potential to do more in the future. Coaching boosts performance by making clear to employees what they should do and how they should best do it ("instruction"), positively reinforcing good work ("praise"), and finding ways to redesign employees' jobs or increase their contribution ("empower").

Mentoring is a subset of coaching, not a matter of semantics. When you mentor top performers, you coach them to take on tasks and responsibilities beyond those designated in their job descriptions; in other words, not only to do their current jobs well. Managers share their experience, wisdom, political savvy, and professional contacts to sustain mentees' motivation, maximize their contribution to the organization, demonstrate interest in their professional growth and development, and help them advance their careers. Once there was an informal relationship between a mentor and his or her mentee, but increasingly mentoring efforts are becoming formalized, a means of helping employees reach their full potential. There are mentoring initiatives to orient new hires, to conserve and transfer special know-how (intellectual capital), to advance the interests of special groups (like women to break the glass ceiling), and to overcome the isolation that diversity of the workforce can create. Sometimes mentoring is one-on-one, sometimes it is done in a group setting; an individual may have more than one mentor, each with unique expertise.

Note that coaching and mentoring are very different from counseling although many of the same steps are involved. Like coaching and often mentoring, counseling is frequently one-on-one, but counseling, unlike coaching and mentoring, is designed to turn around poor performance. Coaching is designed to prevent performance problems from even beginning, stimulating employee commitment from the first day on the job.

Coaching and mentoring recognize that employee growth or development doesn't just happen. It takes a conscious, concerted effort on the part of both managers and employees. Beyond that, it takes time and commitment. When we talk about supporting employee development, we are not advocating once-a-year talks following the annual performance review. The best employee development is ongoing – which means at least monthly coaching. Comparable to the work of a professional coach, managerial coaching involves not only assessment of development needs and subsequent training but also making good hires to begin with. Good coaches recruit only the best, and they train newcomers to close whatever skill gaps remain and more experienced workers to update their skills and increase their employability. Coaches also communicate organization values and mission to ensure that staff are prepared to be empowered and even to share leadership responsibilities.

When you mentor, you become role model, coach, broker, and advocate for your out performers to sustain their motivation despite limited opportunities for advancement, as well as to give them opportunities to utilize their abilities both to their own benefit and to that of the organization.

Done right, mentoring one employee can motivate not only that person but also the remainder of your staff as you demonstrate that you truly care for your employees.

Why mentor and coach? Aside from the corporate advantages, there is a personal benefit. Organizations want managers and HR professionals who can recruit capable employees, develop the skills they need to do today's jobs, and prepare them to handle tomorrow's jobs as well, and who can keep superstars shining even when there is little opportunity for advancement or dollars for increased performance.

Definitions of Terms

In this chapter you will learn:

» the difference between coaching and mentoring.
» the importance of feedback – constructive feedback – to coaching and mentoring;
» the different roles that mentors play; and
» the responsibilities of managers as coach and mentor.

The best way to begin a discussion of any subject is with a definition of terms. In this chapter, you will discover:

» how coaching differs from mentoring, and both differ from counseling;
» coaching's role in another, broader people process: performance management;
» the various corporate approaches to mentoring.

Any confusions you may have about coaching and mentoring should disappear after reading this chapter.

To begin with, coaching and counseling are often thought to be the same. They are not. Nor are coaching and mentoring. The differences among the three lies in their purpose.

Coaching is the process by which managers boost employee performance by making clear to them what they should do and how they should best do it (think "instruction"), positively reinforce good work (think "praise"), and find ways to redesign employees' jobs or increase their contribution (think "empowerment"). Managerial coaching is very similar to sports coaching in that it involves careful selection of good hires, then assessment of development needs and subsequent training and regular feedback.

As coach, a manager acts as a "tutor," detecting and closing gaps in the employee's knowledge or addressing subject matter difficulties the employee is having. The coach will conduct a training assessment or analysis of the skills a job demands and then measure the employee's competencies against the results, in the process identifying gaps to be filled via training – classroom instruction and/or on-the-job learning, including e-learning. This process is done with newcomers, on their first day as part of their orientation or induction into the organization, but it is a process that should be repeated over time to ensure that all hires have the skills they need to do their jobs well.

The result is solid performance, up to or above standard.

But increased job performance isn't the sole benefit of coaching. When employees receive regular feedback, their manager doesn't have to worry about his or her employees being surprised and defensive at performance appraisal time. And the rapport between the manager and employees that coaching creates helps reduce conflicts and complaints.

Everything should run more smoothly – or at least as well as it can in today's lean organizations in which it sometimes seems that firefighting is often the order of the day.

Coach Don Shula said, "Whether it's sports or business, winning and losing doesn't depend on trick plays or new systems. It comes down to motivating people to work hard and prepare to play as a team that really counts. In a word, it's coaching." Actually, regularly scheduled coaching sessions can boost both individual and department or division performance.

Unfortunately, the hard work of a department can be undone by just one staff member who doesn't carry his or her weight. Work output – that is, work done – may be poor or below standard. Due dates for completed assignments may be missed, affecting workflow or the work of others down the line. Then counseling is called for.

Counseling is similar to coaching in that it involves one-on-one meetings between a manager and his or her employee, but the purpose here is to alert the employee that his or her work is sub-par, and continued sub-standard work could subject the employee to dismissal for cause. Records of instances of poor performance – referred to as "critical incident reports" – are used to demonstrate to the employee the gap between actual performance and anticipated performance. The problem may be due to any of a number of problems, from lack of motivation to a poor work attitude, to a training need, to a personal problem that distracts the employee from his or her job.

Whereas counseling is concerned with helping troubled or troublesome employees, and coaching is designed to help new and average employees to develop themselves professionally and become more effective in their jobs, mentoring is designed to help one's best performers utilize their abilities to their benefit and that of the organization. Dr LeRoy T. Walker, president emeritus of the US Olympic Committee, said, "Mentoring is the key to inspiring championship performances."

Mentoring is a topic that is getting much attention today. Ambitious managers and employees are looking for executives and other managers who will agree to help them up a career ladder that has fewer rungs than it had in the past owing to our flatter organizations. These individuals are looking for managers and executives who will cheer them up with "pep talks;" instruct them about the power and political framework of the organization; facilitate projects that they are working on by making both resources and contacts, both with and outside the organization, available; and influence the powers to be to give them a promotion when a vacancy opens up.

When a manager mentors his or her own employees, that manager generally is helping to keep his or her plateaued top performers motivated and talented newcomers more productive sooner. This is closer to its original purpose, which had a senior person acting as a role model and adviser to someone junior to help that person advance in his or her career. But increasingly the definition of mentoring has broadened. The term is even being used as a synonym for the word "partnership," describing a situation in which management of a bigger company offers resources and contacts to a smaller firm's management team under the auspices of a government agency.

Further, whereas mentoring between individuals was often by happenstance, mentoring is being institutionalized. The reasons vary. In academic environments, older students work with younger ones to acclimate the latter to college life or ensure that they do well in school. Sometimes students are mentored by those already employed, with the objective of encouraging the young person to work for his or her mentor's organization upon graduation. Recent graduates are mentored by those in the same field with job experience to speed the new hires' assimilation into the organization. In-country mentors are defined as those individuals who help globally mobile businesspeople adapt to unfamiliar cultures, mores, and legal codes.

Cross-gender mentoring is exactly what it sounds like. Either males or females mentor protégés of the other sex to overcome sexual stereotypes. Cross-cultural mentoring is a reaction to today's diverse workplace. Generally mentors of one ethnic background advise protégés of another culture or background.

Managerial mentors – often the supervisors of the mentees – serve four roles: role model – behaving as they expect their protégés to behave; coach – clarifying the organization's culture, political structure, and vision to encourage their protégés to correctly direct their efforts and avoid the political traps that could derail them from a fast track; broker – clearing the path for their protégés to enable them to reach those whose approval they need; and advocate – becoming cheerleaders for their mentees.

How are these roles performed?

For one, mentees may "shadow" their mentors; that is, they may follow their mentor about as they go about their regular work routine. The technique is particularly beneficial when the mentor finds it difficult to put in words how he or she accomplishes something. In "trialling," a mentee tests an idea or process in a pilot project. Using "job rotation," the protégé may be given the opportunity to hold various jobs and thereby gain more experience than he or she would gather from a single job. A mentor may work with many mentees at one time, thereby serving as a "mentoring hub," or several mentors can support a single protégé, each sharing their expertise. Some mentors look at their protégés as "empty vessels," without the skills, knowledge, and experience that the mentor has accumulated. The role of the mentor is to transmit these abilities to the protégé. Other mentors regard the mentee as a "plant" with the capacity to grow with nurturing. Still other thinkers see the protégé as "the patient," someone who needs to be fixed up professionally. The mentor sees himself or herself as "caregiver," responsible for the professional wellbeing of the protégé. Finally, some mentors see their protégés as "explorers," discovering their own route to personal or professional success with some help from their mentor guide.

The term "contract" is frequently used in describing both mentoring and coaching relationships. A "performance contract" is a document that a manager, as a coach, prepares for each of his or her employees, in which the manager describes the goals he or she expects the employee to achieve. This could be part of the company's formal performance management system that is designed to stimulate high performance or it may be a sheet of paper in which a manager writes down the level of stretch he or she expects of individual employees. A mentoring agreement specifies the role and responsibilities of both the mentor and mentee in their pairing.

If there is a word common to both coaching and mentoring, it is "feedback," which is an objective assessment of the coached person's or mentee's performance, with constructive advice for continuous improvement. After all, that is the reason for coaching and mentoring – continuous performance improvement.

Evolution

This chapter covers the historical evolution of coaching and mentoring. You can also learn:

» how today's view of coaching isn't limited to tutoring; it's part of performance management;
» how senior executives have their personal coaches to help overcome their managerial shortcomings;
» how mentoring has individual and organizational purposes in the twenty-first century; and
» about the creation of corporate-run mentoring programs that supplement more traditional informal mentoring relationships.

Coaching and mentoring are two of the oldest means of human development. Here you will learn:

» the roots of coaching and mentoring;
» the application of coaching and mentoring over the years; and
» today's use of coaching and mentoring

Coaching and mentoring have similar roots and can be traced as far back as the Stone Age when older members of the tribe or clan taught youngsters how to hunt, gather, and prepare food and fight off enemies. Selected younger members were trained by talented cave artists, shamans, and healers to ensure that those skills were perpetuated.

Such sharing of knowledge might equate to an early version of one-on-one knowledge management. Coaching and mentoring follow the old adage (by Confucius): "Give a man a fish, and the man will eat for a day. Teach the man to fish and he will eat for a lifetime."

By definition, coaching is about one-on-one instruction, but in practice it is part of performance management, providing ongoing feedback for the purpose of sustaining and even improving employee performance. It is different from counseling, which addresses specific problems in performance. Coaching is also often confused with mentoring since coaching is an element of mentoring. But mentoring is the process by which a loyal, wise, and helpful friend, teacher, protector, or guide uses his or her experience to show a person how to overcome difficulties and avoid dangers. The original perception of a mentor – a "he" rather than "she" – was as a protector or sponsor, which explains the use of the medieval term "protégé" (literally, "the protected one") to describe the mentee.

The first use of the term is found in Homer's *Odyssey*. The mythical figure, Mentor, was undoubtedly drawn from the real life of his time, however. Often an older man served as advisor to a younger man. In *The Odyssey*, Odysseus, king of Ithaca, went to fight in the Trojan War and entrusted the care of his household and training of his son, Telemachus, to Mentor. For 10 years, Mentor taught Telemachus not solely how to rule but also the values he would need as a man. Odysseus wandered vainly for 10 years in an effort to return home.

When Telemachus grew up, he went in search of his father accompanied, according to Homer's tale, by the goddess Athena, who had assumed the form of Mentor. Eventually father and son were united, and together they fought off the nobles who sought Odysseus' throne and Telemachus' birthright.

Mentoring – from the Greek word meaning 'to counsel' – is defined as a sustained relationship between a youth and an adult. Through continued involvement, the adult offers support, guidance, and assistance as the younger person goes through a difficult period, faces new challenges, or works to solve earlier problems.

Throughout history, there have always been individuals, scattered through all societies, who invested personal time to help others achieve more than they would have without that assistance. Some of these relationships have gone down in history, like Socrates and Plato, Haydn and Beethoven, and Freud and Jung. The fathers of western philosophy regarded the transmission of experience as nothing more than a moral duty. Socrates, for instance, declared that knowledge is the most valuable thing a person can have and that it must be shared for the good of the community.

This relationship of older teacher to student can be found not only in ancient Greece. Indeed, it appears throughout the ages. By the Middle Ages, a system had developed whereby apprentices learned their trades under masters who had gone through the same process themselves. Sometimes the masters were related to their apprentices, but more often they were not relatives but skilled artisans who shared their skills with the youths in return for near-free labor. For centuries, apprenticeship was virtually the only method by which advanced technical skills and knowledge were shared. In essence, the master craftsman "coached" (think "taught") the apprentice how to do one or another task. That craftsman could have been illiterate but it didn't matter – his teachings were through practice rather than book learning.

Apprenticeships were not limited to manual labor. Mentoring occurred also in religious orders. Medicine and law and government were all taught in the same way: a senior practitioner taught his junior.

That model has still not changed as we enter the twenty-first century. Apprenticeship is still a chief form of technical training, with formal apprenticeships replaced with vocational training. Indeed, where certified competence is required, modern versions of apprenticeship can be found. For one, medical interns and law students are expected to work for a certain period of time under senior practitioners before they are considered fully qualified. In universities, senior professors play the classic mentor's role with graduate students, sharing their knowledge and judgment to help in the completion of master's and doctorate papers. And we can't forget the mentoring role played by members of the clergy, social workers, and concerned volunteers who act as mentors to help people to cope with a variety of personal problems.

In sports, coaching is a full-time job, with the coach recruiting team members, helping athletes to perfect their skills, advising on personal problems that interfere with performance on the field, and directing performance to achieve excellence. But coaching extends well beyond the sports arena. Professional coaching is a fundamental element in any winning game plan.

Today's view of coaching evolves from the field of adult development which arose in the late 1950s. Although earlier work by psychologists like Sigmund Freud, Alfred Adler, Carl Gustav Jung, Erik H. Erikson, and Roger Gould pointed to the role that a coach could play in reframing people's thinking as they moved from one phase of human development to another, it was the study of normal and extraordinary growth and development of adults that led to thousands of professionals applying developmental psychology to guide people through meaningful and successful transitions. In the business world, the purpose is to instill a sense of optimism and hope and to give employees and managers the tools they need to evolve and to perform at higher levels – and to become more competent on the job. This coaching role is assumed either by managers/executives or "professional coaches," like HR managers or consultants who practice "executive coaching," working with senior managers to improve their soft people skills.

What about mentoring? Just as in the far away past informal mentoring occurred in any community (like those early Stone Age clans or tribes), so it continues to occur in every organization. After all, firms have their own cultures, their own leaders, their own body politic. Remember the earlier model: elders shared their wisdom with those younger than themselves to maintain the wellbeing of the order. Within businesses, this learning is in the form of skills, abilities, and knowledge developed bit by bit, day by day by these leaders – supervisors, managers, and executives.

Until the end of the twentieth century, in most organizations, mentoring was done informally, especially when both mentor and protégé were in white-collar positions. Senior executives would "adopt" talented newcomers or star performers. The nature of the mentoring had several key characteristics.

» *A single-minded focus on career advancement.* Employees sought mentors – within or outside their organization – to speed their professional advancement.
» *The belief that the mentor would be a protector.* The mentor was seen as advocate of the younger person, using his network to support the mentee's upward progress.
» *A desire to clone look-alike, think-alike, act-alike managers.* The mentors sought out those whose aspirations resembled their own at that age. Likewise, their backgrounds – and their gender and culture.
» *A vision of mentoring that was fundamentally elitist.* Mentoring wasn't designed to speed development of younger managers. Rather, it was a strategy to assimilate high-potential personnel into the inner circle of management.
» *Little concern about corporate mission or strategy.* The emphasis was on the mentee's career development, not organization development.
» *A lack of awareness of hidden talent.* People were characterized by what they did, not their potential, and consequently young people who could have profited from mentoring were overlooked, despite their career aspirations, because of managerial blindness to any but specific job holders or university graduates.

This version of mentoring continues in some companies. But at the end of the twentieth century, mentoring took on a very different look and purpose.

To begin with, research pointed to the worth of mentoring relationships in leadership development, leading to renewed interest in it *per se*. As organizations recognized that mentors, to do their job well, had to see the task as more than peripheral to their work, they made it part of managerial jobs. Some companies drive this point home by specifically pairing off junior and senior employees. The importance of mentoring is further emphasized by the provision of training to both mentor and mentee. The purpose of training the mentor is to enable the person to address both short-term situational needs and long-term aspirations. The mentee training helps the younger individual learn how to become a partner with the mentor, take greater accountability for his or her self-development, and make more effective use of what a mentor can teach him or her.

Note the use of the pronoun "she," as well as "he." Even into the late 1980s, few male managers dared mentor a woman, lest their reputation be tarnished by sexual innuendos. But as companies looked for ways to build high performance managerial and executive teams, they began to practice cross-gender mentoring.

Structured programs may be highly flexible, with mentors and mentees choosing for themselves if they can or should work together. To facilitate such pairing, the organization may maintain an electronic bulletin board system whereby the mentees can list their needs and mentors can identify the talents they could bring to a mentoring relationship. Such systems can allow mentoring relationships to develop at various corporate facilities, even across national boundaries. Of course, there are also much more structured mentoring programs. For instance, there are some organized under the direction of a single manager, sometimes called a "mentoring coordinator," who identifies appropriate matches and is available to support either mentor or mentee when the need arises. There are even programs that allow protégés to evaluate their mentors and mentors to appraise the efforts of their mentees.

Some mentoring relationships include a written contract or agreement that specifies the role of each party and the mentee's learning or performance objectives. Once those objectives have been met, the relationship may be terminated unless a new contractual relationship is set. If either party is dissatisfied with the other in a mentoring relationship, the agreement can be voided and the parties can seek out others. Sometimes mentors ask out. Sometimes it is the mentees.

Although there have been questions raised about these formal programs, contesting that they violate a key principle in mentoring – that is, self-selection – arguing that few formal programs have succeeded, increasingly such relationships are the foundation of programs that extend beyond their initial purpose: individual excellence. As participation in mentoring has grown, companies are now using it to a variety of ends.

» *Advance the interests of special groups and populations.* Whereas in the past mentors selected protégés who looked, thought, and acted as they did, the new organizational mentoring initiatives are designed to help members of select groups rise in the organizations. The mentors' purpose is to help women or members of racial, ethnic, and other definable groups upgrade their leadership skills and political savvy and move into managerial positions.

» *Share special know-how.* The purpose is to speed up company and product knowledge and job skills. The loss of all three is possible when a long-term employee or manager leaves to join another company or retires. The worth of such knowledge became evident after the downsizings of the 1980s and early 1990s as companies realized that the layoffs had produced substantial losses in organizational memory and know-how. Those companies with structured programs expect smoother transitions following deep staff cuts due to the economic downturn than they had a decade ago.

Interestingly, mentoring relationships for the purpose of sharing know-how have undergone a twist as understanding of the technology revolution has become critical to corporate competitive advantage. Rather than older, more experienced managers coaching younger employees, just the reverse is occurring. At some companies young technicians are spending time with more senior managers and executives, making these more experienced managers comfortable with the technology and, more important, acquainting them with the Internet and, in the process, helping these executives identify corporate opportunities for its application.

» *Satisfy Gen-X demands to participate in decision making.* Earlier mentor relationships saw the young protégés as empty vessels waiting to be filled by their more learned, more knowledgeable seniors. There was no awareness that the mentees possessed knowledge that would benefit either the mentor or his organization. No more. The emphasis on employee participation, empowerment, and team decision making has ended that notion. Not only do those who are being mentored want to voice their opinions, they also demand the right – and companies are increasingly training them to ensure that they participate as a partner, proactive in contributing to departmental and organizational problem solving.

» *Support knowledge management.* Mentoring has been found to be an effective way to bring employees together to share good feelings about their work and their workplace. Previous desire to hoard knowledge, skills, and know-how disappears as helping another via mentoring builds goodwill and even friendship. Indeed, for this reason companies encourage a manager to take on more than one mentee, and mentees to have more than one advisor. Companies believe that, over time, mentoring can create many helping relationships and consequently improve the quality of worklife in general and the sharing of best practices specifically.

Indeed, as mentoring contributes to competitive advantage, this would seem to take us full circle back to that first Mentor. In *The Odyssey,* it is Mentor who supplies Telemachus, now grown, with the weapons the young warrior and his father need to battle the usurpers of the father's throne of Ithaca.

TIMELINE

» **Stone Age**: Young cave dwellers learn from their elders how to survive.
» **Ancient Greece**: Young men are tutored by older males in life values, a relationship described by Homer in *The Odyssey* and lived by Plato and Socrates.
» **Middle Ages**: The rise of apprenticeships and later guilds where young, talented men learn from skilled artisans. These same relationships exist in the practice of medicine and religion and later in law.
» **Early 1900s**: Beginning of psychotherapy that provide psychological theories of adult development that serve as half of foundation of coaching as means of adult development and growth, with Sigmund Freud's interpretation of personal life, Alfred Adler's growth model, Carl Jung's belief in rites of passage, and Erik Erikson's turning points.

» **Late 1950s**: Field of adult development arises as an outgrowth of developmental psychology. It begins first as the study of children and adolescents then expands to include adult development – the study of normal and extraordinary growth and development of adults – and subsequent corporate investment in formal training.

» **Late 1950s – early 1960s**: Research by motivational theorists like Maslow and Herzberg and rethinking of the role of manager by researchers like Mintzberg leads to awareness of the role of managers in increasing employee performance.

» **Late 1980s**: Renewed interest in mentoring from brain drain due to waves of downsizing and early retirements triggered by economic downturns.

» **1990s**: Formalized programs in mentoring.

» **Late 1990s–Early 2001**: Corporate programs extend beyond individual excellence to achievement of corporate goals.

The E-Dimension

This chapter covers:

» how ever-changing technology demands regular IT updates;
» how work off site demands a different approach to both coaching and mentoring;
» how computer-based training replaces classroom instruction and supplements on-the-job learning; and
» the nature of reverse mentoring.

The electronic technology that is very much a part of the new millennium has created:

» opportunities to coach and mentor; and
» situations that demand coaching and mentoring.

Let's consider what the electronic revolution has done to the typical office. For one, access to the Internet via the office computer can increase availability of marketing information and corporate best practices to increase competitive advantage, business news, and studies that can identify business opportunities and challenges. But access to the Internet can be misused. Which means lost office productivity. E-mail also can be used to send inappropriate messages that can endanger proprietary information or, depending on the nature of the message, raise charges of sexual harassment or insubordination.

The new office technology has also made it possible for employees to work at home, which demands a whole new means of supervision – and oversight of performance from a distance via e-mail and the telephone. The importance of the new technology to companies has also created two other challenges. First, there is the importance of IT personnel, to the point that in good times they could write their own job ticket, stay briefly, then move on to another position that offered more opportunity for training, work/family balance, and dollars. Even as the economy has dipped downward, IT personnel remain in great demand. While other workers worry about finding another job if they are downsized, their IT counterparts are seeking out more secure positions in other firms – and, depending on the knowledge they bring to a new employer, are likely to get a positive reception.

Fortunately, the Internet has become a source for a greater pool of job candidates, particularly IT personnel. Corporate Websites have also become a tool for recruitment. And hiring the very best is one of the responsibilities of a manager in the position of coach.

The new technology has also raised business questions that demand knowledge about the Internet and specific hardware and software that senior executives lack. Consequently, opportunities for new distribution channels are lost and money is spent unwisely as IT personnel press for the latest technology rather than the most necessary technology. But more progressive companies have found that mentoring by the IT personnel of their technologically illiterate senior executives can be a fast means of getting these top executives up to speed on the opportunities available to the firm from the new business technology.

Indeed, the new technology itself has become a means of instruction that minimizes time away from the office. Right now, while some feel uncomfortable about business travel, access to e-based learning is a convenient way to train employees on both hard and soft skills.

Office technology has created challenges for businesses but it has also created opportunities to address them. Let's look in greater detail at these solutions.

On the simplest level, the new technology speeds the coaching/ mentoring process – bringing it up to dot-com time. Mentors and protégés or coaches and coached need not wait to exchange information. Rather, they can communicate via e-mail or voicemail, intranet or Internet. And let's not forget cell phone.

Electronic communication has proven to be as effective as face-to-face communication. A manager can e-mail an answer or advice on a work problem rather than schedule a meeting and then wait to hold that meeting. There is even software that sets up discussion boards where employees can have ongoing dialogues with their coaches or mentors.

Electronic communication also allows coaching and mentoring relationships to exist in which those involved work in different locations – not only in different offices but in different countries. Thanks to electronic technology, a mentor can be in one part of the world and communicate with a protégé in another part of the world. The technology also allows managers to be mentors to individuals outside their company – from disadvantaged youngsters who need positive role models to talented students studying to enter the same field. In Florida, as a case in point, managers – from CEOs to employees – volunteer to mentor youngsters for an hour a week. Under direction of Governor Bush, the program has drawn over 250 companies from different industries to participate in a program as dependent on e-mail mentoring as face-to-face communications.

In Austin, Texas, of 3000 mentors for high school students, 300 are e-mentors. There are another 1000 tech workers on a waiting list for next year's mentoring program. The employees come from a diverse group of businesses, including Austin Energy, IBM, and the University of Texas. Through regular e-mails, the technology-minded grown-ups keep in touch with grade-school students and try to reinforce the value of education.

Direct Contact Online Volunteers (www.serviceleader.org) is one of many Websites that seek out volunteer mentors, tutors, advisors, and others to work with clients (including students) for a variety of purposes, from "visiting" someone who is homebound, to providing online mentoring and instruction (like helping a student with a homework question or a young adult learn a skill or find a job), help people learn English as a second language, manage a support line, provide advance "welcomes" to people about to enter hospital, go to summer camp and the like or offer post-service follow-up, and train others for free via the Internet.

When it comes to telecommuting, communications between managers and employees can be electronic but it also can be in person. Indeed, as coach of a telecommuter, a manager needs to meet in person as well as communicate via e-mail and telephone with the off site worker.

Distance management, as it has been called by some authors, is little different from supervision of employees on site. Likewise, coaching. Among the responsibilities are the following.

» *Set clear expectations*. The coach and coached both have to have a clear idea of what each job is to achieve. Standards are in writing. Indeed, coach and coached – like mentor and mentee in their relationship – may want to spell out the telecommuter's and manager's responsibilities.

» *Agree on performance standards*. What will a good job look like? When the coach talks to the telecommuter, either online or in person, he or she should have measurements as quantifiable as possible.

» *Agree on how results will be monitored*. Since the manager, in the role of coach, can't look outside his or her door to see how busy the staff member is, agreement on how work will be measured is critical. What reporting methods will be used – written or verbal reports, computer tracking, phone, or face-to-face meetings? How frequent will these be?

» *Monitor Internet activity*. It's very easy for remote workers to become Internet junkies, caught up in the information superhighway. So coaches need to include in standards what level of use will be considered an abuse of the communications technology.

» *Provide feedback on performance*. A manager will conduct regular performance assessments, but periodic coaching sessions should also be held in which feedback is given. If a real problem exists, then the employee should clearly be called into the office for a face-to-face conversation. But interim progress reports can be handled by telephone or e-mail. To maximize the use of this medium, plan in advance what you will say or write electronically, just as you would think about any firsthand conversation prior to sitting down with an employee.

» *Build trust*. Since distance management doesn't give a coach the same control over teleworkers as they have with employees who work beside him or her, the coach has to rely on the remote control that comes from their respect for the coach. The coach can begin to foster that trust by showing trust himself or herself in the off site employee unless evidence proves otherwise. Operate on the assumption of trust, not distrust. Question only when there is real reason to do so – which is what an outstanding supervisor does anyway.

» *Communicate, communicate, communicate*. I've given this advice elsewhere, but nowhere is it more important than in working with remote workers. Sometimes you may have to contact a remote worker in the role of coach three or four times a day. Identify e-points or talking points in a list that you keep with you during the communications. Fine tune, too, your "listening" skills. In telementoring, give what is said your full attention. In your e-mail, think first before you press the "Send" button with your message.

» *Set up technical support systems for remote workers*. As a coach, you want to be sure that those workers off site are not hindered by lack of resources from doing the job you've hired them to do.

Help teleworkers build camaraderie so that they will lean on one another despite the physical distance between them. If you are too busy to fully complete your mentoring or coaching responsibilities, then you may want to identify a buddy on site or within the same neighborhood as that of a new teleworker. This way, your new hire will have both technological and emotional support. Don't stop at one buddy, either. Encourage all members of your team to communicate with one another as well as with you. Encourage a little informal networking so that members of the group who are off site stay in touch via e-mail messages not only with those in the office but also with others like them who work from home.

Let's look at another issue tied to the new office technology: the need for senior management to know more about the new office technology. The solution has become so popular that it even has a name – "reverse mentoring." Generally, executives are mentored by IT professionals who coach them in the use of the technology. Some executives seek out a counterpart in another company – even in the high-tech field itself – to coach them (see "Reverse Mentoring" below). Mentoring senior executives in the use of technology begins with the basics: search engines, Web-based e-mail, news Websites, and multimedia. The training goes on to subjects like B2C shopping, protocol in chat rooms, instant messaging, resources for technology news (to stay abreast of trends and developments), and Web page design and hosting.

Finally, the programs move to advanced subjects like Web content personalization, business commerce, participation in business chat rooms, new business models, B2B opportunities, wireless services, database applications accessible via Internet, such as customer relationship management and supply chain management, and even people management, including compensation, personnel records, etc.

In an increasingly accelerated workplace, we must take control of the technology. As coach for your department team, create policies and etiquette for using e-mail, voicemail, and other collaborative systems. Employees should know, for example, when to mark a message urgent, an acceptable time frame for replying or calling back, and what's not allowed in e-mail, including sensitive HR information, jokes and chain letters, and banal comments.

Technology is itself a means to address learning needs. E-learning continues to be on the increase. While classroom instruction continues to be popular, the cost of travel has prompted companies to investigate and implement e-training initiatives. In his or her role as coach, a manager will need to assess training needs and determine the most efficient and effective training to fill skill gaps. And training off the Web shouldn't be neglected as a means of learning. Nor should the use of e-learning be neglected as a means of training to retain the more mobile employees in today's economic downturn. Which takes us to another responsibility of a coach: recruitment.

A coach's role is to hire the very best. And recruitment sites on the Web offer a large pool from which to choose talented employees, particularly IT personnel. HR professionals and managers have found that recruitment via the Web can speed the time it takes to fill a vacancy. Electronic technology can be used to scan resumés received electronically and then these resumés can be collected, to be used when the need arises. Or, given the vast number of resumés that Web recruiting generates, office technology can be used to screen incoming resumés and identify those candidates most likely to succeed in the job.

In their role as coach, managers will also want to speak to their IT professionals about the corporate Website. The site itself should be designed to gather resumés from those who visit - regardless of area of expertise. Coaches should look at their Website as a platform on which to present their company in the best light, from training opportunities once employed to compensation plans to opportunities for empowerment and high visibility.

So the new office technology has made the role of coach more complex and more simple simultaneously.

REVERSE MENTORING

Unfortunately it's true: those new to management - even new hires - are more familiar with the electronic technology than our middle and senior managers. Indeed, many senior executives feel overwhelmed by the technology. They recognize its importance but they depend on others for advice to make decisions about its use - not always the best solution, since many technical persons aren't familiar with the broader picture. GE's Jack Welch faced this problem and solved it using a technique that has become known as "reverse mentoring;" that is, instead of senior personnel mentoring younger staff members, senior executives are coached by younger employees in a specific issue or topic. In the case of GE, it was 1000 executives and the topic was technology.

The process at GE required senior managers – including Welch – to spend time learning from Internet and technology experts from within the company. This learning included basic Internet skills, discussing important trends and developments on the Web. Needless to say, critical to the program was the identification of technology-knowledgeable employees who could serve as reverse mentors. They might be young and low ranking in the organization but they had to have the self-confidence to teach the senior executives about technology trends, even insist that senior executives, busy with other business, keep scheduled meetings for the instruction. The instruction began with such basics as how to use an Internet search engine and moved on to more advanced topics like chat rooms and online shopping.

If there was one problem with this initiative it was getting the executives to admit they had a technology problem. For many, it was difficult but it was necessary to get their commitment to ensure they would listen to these younger employees.

What was the benefit? Dollar savings as senior managers maximized the use of the technology and were able to make better decisions when presented by IT with various purchasing options.

Incidentally, Welch took coaching not only from a junior employee on the Internet. He and Sun Microsystems CEO Scott McNealy have regular discussions about management, technology, and other issues. Welch learns about the latest technology developments from McNealy, and McNealy learns how to manage a large corporation from Welch. Which would seem to be another form of mentoring in search of a descriptive name.

The Global Dimension

This chapter explains how:

» US firms trail those from the rest of the world in preparing managers for overseas assignments;
» managers can prepare to be globally and locally focused; and
» nine factors critical to success in assignments can be covered by coaching and/or mentoring.

Signs of cultural diversity are virtually everywhere. This diversity represents some of the most subtle and special relationships imaginable. Even in relatively homogeneous societies, differences in economic class, religious background, regional allegiance, even family traditions can generate cultural differences that can complicate work relationships.

Now consider work relationships that span national borders. In this chapter, you will learn how coaching and mentoring are:

» facilitating ''going global'' by developing cultural astuteness in expatriate managers;
» relying on electronic communications to prepare managers for overseas assignments; and
» making short-term assignments abroad feasible.

As companies operate within a single nation, they have turned to mentoring and coaching to help individuals who are not representative of the ''old boys' network'' to become part of the organization's management team. Likewise, they have developed programs to enable managers from one part of the world to work collaboratively with those from other parts by teaching them, via mentoring and coaching, the national and business cultures of each. Electronic communication enables expatriates to develop the cultural astuteness they need to work effectively abroad. E-mail is the means of communication between mentor and protégé or coach and coached.

In the past, such cultural savvy could have been developed over time. But no more so. Today's marketplace demands that companies have a global workforce that is mobile. A study by New York City-based Organization Resources Counselors Inc. has found the use of short-term assignments on the increase. Overseas assignments of 12 months or fewer averaged 5.3% in 1992 but were at 16% in 1998. According to Geoffrey W. Latta, vice president, the interest is driven by several factors, pure cost being the first. Although HR managers admit that the organization gains are greater if an assignment is longer, given the time it takes to adapt to another national culture, to learn the overseas operations, to become accepted in the new business environment, and thereby operate most effectively, nevertheless experience has shown that a shorter time frame can accommodate certain assignments (e.g. projects) while also saving money.

Employees who lack experience working abroad are also reluctant to take on international assignments. Three to five years – many employees just don't want to be uprooted for such a long period, particularly without any connection to others in their new locale.

As expatriates have less time to adapt to other national cultures, long-distance mentoring and coaching prior to the start of an assignment grow in importance. Global training and development have several benefits, including:

» improved ability to work side by side with nationals;
» sensitivity to viable business opportunities; therefore, less chance of pursuit of an ill-conceived venture; and
» improved job satisfaction and retention of members of the global workforce.

Ideally, training should be very much a part of the responsibility of human resources. Many countries already recognize this. Japan, for one, takes up to three years to prepare a manager for an overseas assignment. A June 1990 survey of 6000 employers in France, Spain, the UK, Sweden, and Germany found that global preparation was perceived as critically important and spreading rapidly. Other countries aren't as perceptive – like the United States. Although $200bn is spent annually in human resource development by the US, 70% of American business people are sent abroad with no cultural training or preparation. 59% of human resource development executives surveyed by the American Society for Training and Development said there was no international training for personnel taking assignments outside the United States, and another 5% didn't even know there was any such training.

What do I mean by a global workforce? It is a staff of employees and managers with the skills, abilities, and knowledge to achieve success in a global arena, a staff made necessary as we increasingly shop the world for markets and business partners. This workforce will have a cosmopolitan outlook; the ability to communicate across cultures and to manage cross-cultural conflict, to negotiate internationally, to work in multicultural teams, and to establish close personal relationships with people from around the world; and the knack to motivate people from a wide range of cultures.

Such ability demands ongoing support – which may be provided by both coaching and mentoring. Where training efforts do not exist, the importance of coaching and mentoring is even greater.

Performance management will depend on training and development, with the emphasis on individuals in their work roles. The primary training will be through on-the-job learning, but coaching – in person and via e-mail – can also support the need for individual learning. Healthy inter-unit and intra-unit relationships will depend on the individual staff member's knack for addressing cultural differences, and will come from experience and, where time is too short to understand cultural diversities, via mentoring by those from the other culture. Structured and informal mentoring efforts will influence the relationship of individuals and groups and in turn impact the successful integration of business units from various parts of the world.

No question, mentoring also provides self-knowledge to those with overseas assignments, alerting them to shortcomings and, more importantly, providing an action plan to address skill gaps.

The challenge in the global arena for managers, as coaches and mentors, is to prepare those under their sponsorship to be both globally and locally focused. Just as domestically coaches and mentors are responsible for guiding those they coach or mentor in order that they have the skills, abilities, and knowledge to succeed in their current jobs or advance into more demanding positions, so globally coaches and mentors are responsible for supporting those they coach or mentor in order that they are able to keep pace with the accelerated change that is so much a part of the global world of work.

Whether the global business entails a joint venture or a partnership, or a merger, or simply a new market for an existing product, there are cultural issues that must be taught. Culture can be described in several ways. It is a way of life shared by all or almost all within an area, that older members of the group pass on to younger members, and that shapes behavior and structures the view of the world. Culture reflects our thinking, doing, and living; that is, it includes our values, beliefs, myths, and folklore; it includes the laws, customs, regulations, ceremonies, fashions, and etiquette by which we live; and it includes our language as well as clothing and tools and food. Geert Hofstede defined culture as "a collective programming of the mind ... It is learned, not inherited. It derives from one's social environment, not from one's genes."

The role of mentors and coaches is to prepare those under their direction with some appreciation of the culture in which they will work, whether the assignment is short- or long-term. That means making protégé or coached alert to nine factors that, acting one upon another, create the culture of a country or region.

What are these nine factors?

1 *Religion*. This may be the single most influential factor in cultural thinking – and thereby living and doing. Religion is the foundation for many beliefs and norms, determining what is most important in life. Many religious writings describe how one should eat, dress, relate to others, and work.

2 *Education*. How knowledge, skills, and attitudes are transmitted is determined by education. Education may be formal (primary, secondary, higher, and vocational), non-formal (structured but not from any academic system, like on-the-job learning), or informal (unstructured, such as learning from one's parents). Some societies encourage rote learning in an environment with complete, absolute respect and obedience to the instructor, while other societies support participative learning with a more egalitarian relationship between teacher and student.

3 *Economics*. Societies may be capitalistic, government controlled, or a combination of both. Recent events in Eastern Europe, Asia, and Africa show a rapid movement even in these formerly centrally planned economic systems toward a more capitalistic, free-market economy, but economists expect the impact of Marxist economics to influence the culture of these societies for many years to come.

4 *Politics*. When we talk about politics, we are talking about both political structures and activities related to the allocation and use of power. Political systems range from totalitarian to democratic and may exclude specific groups based on ethnicity, gender, age, or economic status.

5 *Family*. The concept of family in a culture may range from nuclear (immediate) to extended (including grandparents, cousins, aunts, and uncles). The nuclear family has limited interaction outside the

family members, which means that family members are free to ignore the demands of the extended family but also may mean that family members are free to choose their marriage partners, professions, and living arrangements. In extended families – found in most of Asia, Africa, and Latin America – the obligation to family members overrides the desires and wishes of the individual, which means that all members – but especially the son – are expected to remain with the family to support it in whatever way they can.

6 *Language*. We may not realize so, but the words and structures in our language strongly reflect our values and beliefs. English, for instance, is a very direct and active language. If we like something, we say so. If we don't, we also say so. On the other hand, Japanese is a less direct language, in which opinion is softened. Indeed, communications between the two groups often become confused, as Americans mistake the word "yes" for acceptance rather than acknowledgement that an issue is under consideration.

Not only is English more direct, it is also less formal. In English, for instance, there is only one form of the second person for both singular and plural. In Vietnamese, by contrast, there are many counterparts of "you," and each is dependent upon age, gender, relationship, number, and status.

The consequences in terms of culture should be self-evident. It is more natural for an American to be informal and egalitarian than for a Vietnamese.

7 *Class structure*. In open class structures, people may choose to move up, down, or laterally in the system without major difficulty. Within a closed society, one's position is determined and limited by who one is – that is, by birth rather than by accomplishment. India has a class system that is very closed, whereas the US has a very open class structure.

8 *History*. No question, a society's history impacts its culture. China has a long and glorious history and it has given the Chinese a very different perspective on time than, say, those in a newly formed nation in Africa. Colonized countries of Africa and Asia have many values derived from, and/or in contradiction to, their colonizers. The Arabs identify with the military achievements of Muhammad and his successors. The US takes pride in the rugged western history,

rapid industrialization, and the democratic system that came about following the Declaration of Independence in 1776.

9 *Geography*. The events of September 11, 2001 have clearly demonstrated how different perspectives exist between those whose land is made up of vast farmland, forests, and valuable minerals and those with a scarcity of arable land. Whereas one has contributed to America's optimism and confidence and maybe excessive materialism, the other may perhaps explain the Arab's more fatalistic viewpoint.

Needless to say, culture isn't as simple as the nine factors described above suggest. Most countries have many ethnic cultures within their borders. Cameroon has as many as 100. And, surprisingly, Los Angeles County in the United States, according to the last US Census, has 150. Sri Lanka has two distinct ethnic groups. There are also regional similarities in culture. Some cultural factors are so powerful that they influence many nations within the region, as is the case throughout Latin America and the Middle East. Some people of the world live in nations whose borders appear to have kept out all diversity, but a review of their history usually finds that other cultures were driven out in the past.

Finally, any discussion of culture demands discussion of corporate culture. Each organization has a distinct culture that is passed down from older to newer members of the organization and determines management's thinking. Every organization works in some way differently from every other organization. As companies are acquired by other organizations, this factor, too, must be considered. Mentoring or coaching can prepare an employee to adapt to the demands of the change it brings.

The State of the Art

In this chapter, discover:

» how coaching and mentoring programs work;
» how executive coaching is believed to yield six times its cost;
» the traits that make the best coaches;
» the characteristics to look for in mentors;
» concerns proponents of mentoring have about structured programs;
» what makes for good feedback, whether for coaching or mentoring; and
» the traps in mentoring and coaching.

Both coaching and mentoring have experienced renewed interest.

Membership of the International Coach Federation (ICF), Washington, DC, has grown 600 percent since 1997, to over 3000 members. More interestingly, new members are joining at the rate of about 100 each month. Experts estimate there are 10,000 corporate coaches worldwide. According to a survey by Manchester Inc., an HR consulting firm based in Jacksonville, Florida, 59 percent of organizations currently offer coaching or other developmental counseling to their managers and executives. Not only are companies offering coaches to managers, but managers are asking for them. At one time, the need for a coach might be an indictment of one's poor management style. But more recently, managers and executives have come to recognize how a coach, internal or external, can identify their strengths and weaknesses, set goals, and discover creative answers to ongoing operational problems. Perhaps, to some extent, the interest shown by executives and managers in having their own coach may be a result of the use of 360-degree feedback programs within companies that have identified unexpected interpersonal shortcomings.

Whereas companies increasingly are either hiring full-time internal coaches or contracting with personnel consultants to serve as executive coaches to their senior staff, there is also greater recognition about the coaching role that managers play in their employees' job success. Since coaching is a method of providing training as well as ongoing feedback, it fits naturally into the times, when there is so much interest in the value of ''learning organizations'': that is, companies that recognize the worth of acquiring knowledge and acquiring skills as competitive advantage. There is a problem with coaching as it is practiced in many companies. However, there is much more talk about the worth of coaching, even when it is supposedly measured as part of supervisors' annual performance appraisals, than there is effort to prepare managers to coach effectively. Too often, managers fail as coaches because they have had no formal training in it.

Getting employees to change their behavior is not an easy task. It takes sensitivity to provide constructive feedback. But without suitable training, most supervisors do what they are most comfortable doing: tell ... Tell ... YELL! The problem with this approach should be self-evident. The problem is that all it does is alienate the employee.

The problem with telling someone they have to change is two-fold: First, there is no guarantee that the employee will accept that there is a problem. Second, and more important, most employees become defensive when they are told they are doing something in one way that could be done more efficiently in another way. The best way to gain support for the need to change, as the best supervisory coaches know, is to ask questions, rather than give answers.

A further problem with too many corporate efforts at coaching is the confusion about coaching's use. Too often, it is seen not as an ongoing process but merely as the means to address troublesome job performance. Too often, coaching gets confused with counseling or the process of turning around problem performance, probably because a form of coaching is a part of the counseling process. Too often, too, coaching is seen as tied to the performance appraisal process, as something done at quarterly reviews or the end-of-the-year assessment, rather than as the more pervasive feedback that begins when employees come on board, and is provided on a regular basis or as needed, with a strong skill training element to it.

Done well, coaching can boost not only individual performance but also organizational effectiveness. Poorly done, it can alienate employees and undermine performance. What are some of the mistakes that supervisors make today as coaches?

In general, despite exhortations that people are their most important resource, many supervisors fail to treat them as such. Which translates to their indifference in addressing these people's need for support and nurturing or for additional training and advice. When we have an employee who isn't doing what he or she is supposed to do, we tend to attack the employee's personality, not address the situation, thereby doing the exact opposite of what the employee needs to change the undesirable behavior.

When supervisors encounter problems with machines, materials, facilities, or budgets, they take the time to figure out ways to improve their performance. Take the simple example of the computer on your desk. If it weren't working, you would, at the very least, contact the Information Technology department to send someone to fix it. In contrast, when employees demonstrate shortcomings, many supervisors ignore the problem, pointing to the high stack of paperwork and other tasks they need to complete themselves as their excuse. They absolve themselves of all responsibility to address the problem, even if over the long term it means the loss of a potentially good employee and the cost of recruitment. Think again about that computer on your desk. It would be almost like looking at that machine that isn't operating as it should and concluding that "The problem is the machine's fault. There's nothing I can do about it," then pushing it aside until it is replaced by a new model.

When it comes to outstanding work by employees, too many managers would agree with the sentiment of one supervisor I know who told me that she had too much to do to *waste time* on praise.

Admittedly, we managers have lots to do and little time to get it done. Unfortunately, that is not sufficient excuse to be blind to staff shortcuts or other less-than-perfect efforts. Unfortunately, when we ignore these small problems, they can grow to the point that they are no longer coaching problems but issues for counseling. Likewise, acknowledgement of outstanding performance. Acknowledging good performance doesn't have to mean big dollars. Recognition for positive behavioral change can come in the form of praise and other positive reinforcement. Unless you acknowledge performance improvements as you encounter them, no matter how small they may be, these small improvements aren't likely to be permanent. Nor are they likely to be followed by bigger improvements over time.

In his or her role as coach, the well-trained manager begins from the first day that an employee is on board. Indeed, coaching begins even before, by hiring the most qualified for a job. Often, all it takes to identify people with the potential to do good to outstanding work is to hold lengthier interviews with applicants, ask more targeted questions to learn about job skills, attitudes, and past results, and schedule follow-up interviews with other interviewers. Multiple interviewers generally increase the range of questions as well as provide a variety of perspectives for consideration of applicants.

Once a good employee is on board, these same good coaches know to devote time to orienting the employee. Coaches who neglect to orient an employee or postpone orientation soon find themselves with a potentially effective employee whose work is starting to flounder. The employees are off track because no one has taken the time to put them on the right track by making clear the performance level expected or filling skill gaps first identified during recruitment.

A needs analysis should be conducted, and a training effort should be agreed upon to fill competency gaps.

Thereafter, the degree of coaching depends on the individual. While I recommend coaching on a periodic basis, at least practice coaching based on the degree of direction your employees need, taking into account their experience and self-confidence and the nature and importance of the task assigned. In a sense, use the concept of situational management to gauge the degree of coaching each and every one of your employees needs. The same approach should be followed with coaching, regardless of the situation; that is, the communication should be open and honest. And let me add another demand: respectful. Employees should be treated with dignity and respect. Too often, when managers have an employee who is not doing what he or she is expected to do, they tend to respond in ways that aggravate, not help, the situation. Some managers will take an employee's personality: "You are not motivated" or "You are not ambitious" or "You are too ambitious" or "You are careless." Some supervisors will bang doors, slam down phones, even throw things, aggressive responses they would never practice in dealing with a senior executive or tolerate from an employee.

Suggesting that someone is not motivated or argumentative or uninterested in his or her work is demoralizing, more likely to decrease the individual's level of performance than otherwise.

Coaching takes patience. When coaches become emotional over a stupid mistake they send a message to their employees that they "can't believe just how stupid they are." Patience sends a very different message – it tells employees that the coach recognizes that they are human beings and, as such, they have human fallibility, yet there is no reason to quit. As human beings, they also have the capability to improve their performance, and their manager will work with them to see that becomes a reality.

The same message should be sent by mentors to protégés during mentoring sessions.

Just as interest in coaching has grown due to increased pressure for higher performance, so, too, has interest in mentoring. Initially the means by which a more senior person helped a junior individual to advance in his or her career, it has become a tool to retain high performers and to more fully utilize their skills, abilities, and knowledge. Mentoring programs themselves have gone from being informal relationships to help the junior party, to being corporate initiatives designed to grow the skills of both mentor and protégé, to being structured programs designed for corporate purposes as well as the growth of the participants.

Mentoring doesn't just take place in the business community. A review of the many programs out there is fascinating. A review of just some gives some idea of the variety.

» *YWCA Mentoring Program (Vancouver, British Columbia)*. This program partners young women from local secondary schools with professional women who act as female role models and who offer support and guidance regarding education and future career choices to their mentees.

» *Chamber of Commerce (Coquitiam, British Columbia)*. The Education Committee invites high school students, through the schools' Career Prep classes, to the Chamber's monthly business meetings, where a businessperson is assigned to act as mentor through the meeting, introduce them to people, put them at ease, and answer their questions.

» *Pratt & Whitney Canada, Ltd. (Longueuil, Quebec)*. This corporation offers three mentoring programs: one, called Jeunes Entrepreneurs, includes youth in schools across Canada who may be interested in careers in technology; the second program targets two youths each year who have quit school, youngsters in trouble who can benefit from extra time with an adult; and the third program involves 200 students annually who receive as much as two hours of coaching per day as well as a written report.

» *Hewlett-Packard (Online)*. HP offers its e-mail mentor program to grades 5–12 students and teachers with a focus on helping the students to excel in math and science. The mentors are all employees of HP and all the mentoring is provided online.

» *Management Leadership for Tomorrow (New York City, New York)*. This is a nonprofit organization committed to helping students of color across the US plan their careers in business during their early years in college. The program provides mentors to help students increase their eligibility for MBA programs, learn tips about how to excel on admission tests, and how to find financial resources.

» *Eaton Corporation (Cleveland, Ohio)*. Now in its sixth year, the Eaton Minority Engineering Scholars Program pairs undergrads pursuing BS degrees in electrical, mechanical, industrial, or environmental engineering or computer science with senior technical people who guide them through the summer season and keep in touch during the school year as well.

» *Service Corps of Retired Executives (Delray Beach, Florida)*. A volunteer network of retired executives, SCORE provides mentoring to people in business throughout the US. The program is funded by the US Small Business Administration and is located in major cities across the United States.

» *Prairie Records (Halstad, Minnesota)*. Students are connected with adult mentors working in agricultural businesses (farmers, soil and water conservation districts, and chemical applicators).

» *Mentorship Overseas (Spangdahlem, Germany)*. At Spangdahlem Air Base in Germany, middle school students are matched with US Air Force mentors who help them with their studies. The goal is to build student self-esteem and bolster academic performance. The volunteers spend one hour per week with the students helping them with their reading, math, and science assignments. A teacher at the school is also the mentorship coordinator. Teachers and parents nominate students for the mentorship program. Once a student's parents give permission, a mentor volunteer is matched with a student. Students with mentors complete a survey to determine their interests. The mentors are also asked which grade level they prefer, what their strengths are, and are matched with students they can help the most.

» *Business Success Teams (Vancouver, British Columbia)*. A roundtable type of mentoring program, groups of entrepreneurial members meet twice monthly to assist one another in identifying and solving business challenges. Each team has a facilitator, and guests are invited to speak.

» *Job Corps (Columbia, South Carolina)*. The US Department of Labor Job Corps program provides mentoring at two levels. In the admissions office and on campus, there is both a formal and an informal orientation to the company and its procedures. The work requires a great deal of teamwork, so they encourage as much mentoring and networking as possible. They also encourage the same kind of mentoring within the student population. New arrivals on campus are assigned a big brother/sister to acquaint them with the campus, activities, schedules, etc.

» *UConn Mentor Connection (Storrs, Connecticut).* A summer program for high school juniors and seniors, the program has faculty mentors matched with students who work on a variety of projects and activities related to their studies.

» *New Start Center for Learning (Worcester, Massachusetts).* Every school morning begins with a mentoring period between student and teacher mentor. The goal of this at-risk-youth program is to identify any difficulties a student may have had in the last 24 hours or through the weekend. The mentor period lasts 20 minutes in the morning, and an additional mentor time occurs after lunch that lasts for 15 minutes. The purpose of twice daily mentoring is to form a trusting relationship with each student in order to help the students feel free to speak up, as well as to increase personal and academic success.

» *Texas A&M University Teacher Induction Program (Corpus Christi, Texas).* First-year teachers are encouraged to return to university and meet once a week with their mentors, who are retired teachers. The mentors also observe the novice teachers in their district classrooms. The new teachers also receive support from current teachers in their second semester of the full-year course. The mentors receive training and can also receive course credits toward a graduate degree.

» *Cherry Lane Alternative Mentoring Project (New York, New York).* This falls into the creative category of mentoring programs, pairing master playwrights with aspiring writers on a one-on-one basis. Writers receive the appropriate level of support for a particular play, and can also gain opportunities for rehearsal and performance time as well as marketing and financial support. To be selected, new writers' work is first reviewed by a committee of established playwrights. The scripts of the semi-finalists are then reviewed by those who have volunteered to act as mentors. The mentors read between three and five scripts each, from which they select one. The author is the individual whom they mentor.

» *Orlando Fire Department (Orlando, Florida)*. This program began in 1995 as a cadet training program to encourage members of the community to become firefighters. Because of the intensive and extensive training involved, the department decided to pair each student with a seasoned firefighter who could enhance their training. The two are paired for about six months.

» *Syncrude Canada Ltd. (Fort McMurray, Alberta)*. Succession planning is an essential component of this corporate initiative. As part of its leadership development plan, senior managers identify high-potential employees in their respective areas. Each person then details a development plan that includes work assignments, mentoring, and additional educational opportunities.

» *Royal Bank (throughout Canada)*. To meet diversity goals at the Royal Bank, a pilot mentoring process was launched in 1997 and expanded nationally in 1999 using technology to make the process accessible to all employees in any location. Through telephone keypad access, mentors are able to register on a system the skills they will volunteer to develop with a partner, while the partner registers on the system, indicating the skills they want to develop. The skills identified by the partner are those he or she feels are important either to meet the needs of the business unit the individual is in, or to increase his or her skills to compete for future positions of interest. The organization matches mentors and protégés.

» *Transamerica Intellitech (Sacramento, California)*. New managers are given mentors from a group of senior managers who have volunteered to serve as such. Pairings are done by the organization based on the protégé's completion of a form based on expectations for the mentoring relationship.

» *Metropolitan Transportation Authority (New York, New York)*. The MTA created a program to develop its employees. Called the Future Managers Program, it includes a mentor–participant contract that eliminates some of the confusion in terms of responsibilities of the various participants. Both parties design and sign the contract that indicates when and how they will communicate.

» *Cigna Financial Advisors Partnership Program (San Antonio, Texas)*. A comprehensive recruitment, training, and retention program for new agents, begun in late 1995, gave birth to the firm's Partnership Program. It requires that all new hires work for a period of up to 27 months under the direction of an experienced, successful mentor. Each agency hires only the number of new producers who can be personally trained, supervised, and developed by qualified, experienced producers or sales managers.

» *Merck and Company, Inc. (West Point, Pennsylvania)*. Designed for its field sales reps, Merck and Company's mentor program has protégés spend three days with their mentors to learn the ropes. During this period, they also work together on a number of job-related tasks. The company has created a mentor guide with short activities to make it easier for mentor and mentee to get to know each other. The guide also contains information for the mentor on the Merck corporate culture and work values. Mentors are chosen by senior management, based on their coaching capabilities. Once chosen, mentors go through a one-day mentor training program.

» *Procter & Gamble (Cincinnati, Ohio)*. The program at P&G is different from those described so far in that it has lower levels of the business units acting as mentors for those higher up in the business. The mentors are one to two levels below those whom they coach, and the coaching is designed to help these senior executives to develop greater self-awareness of their behavior.

» *Sandia National Laboratories (Albuquerque, New Mexico)*. A formal program, this program was initially created for managers but now is available to all 7500 staff members. The purpose of the program is to enhance career development, improve responsiveness to change, and strengthen response to customer needs. Employees wishing to participate as mentors or mentees attend an orientation and complete a self-assessment. The HR department matches pairs, but individuals can suggest a person with whom to work. Partners then arrange a meeting and complete an agreement that defines the pair's objectives, sets goals, and details roles.

For further examples of mentoring programs, see Chapter 7. You can see some common threads in these programs that suggest their aims. For instance, mentoring is seen as a means to create a pipeline to facilitate the movement of talented women and minority employees into senior management. In *HR Magazine,*Patricia Digh, a business writer/analyst, writes, "Talented women and minority employees sometimes lack the informal networks and savvy that win promotions for their white male colleagues. Mentoring plans may boost recruitment and retention of high-potential employees – of all kinds." Companies have also found that formal mentoring is an excellent means for seasoned executives to share intellectual capital and expertise with promising neophytes. And the programs also serve to facilitate succession planning, ensuring a continuous flow of potential leaders within an organization.

Mentors and protégés no longer fit the traditional pattern. Juniors may mentor seniors, and employees may mentor other co-workers within their organization. Finally, the means of communication is no longer limited to face-to-face meetings. There are real-time group meetings among mentors and their protégés but there are also online meetings and even telephone conferences. Successful use of the telephone for in-depth conversations and the fax machine to send messages has shown that mentoring can be practiced from a distance.

Those organizations that look on mentoring as an organic process – that is, an effort that evolves and grows – seem to have greater success with the concept. Writing for the American Society for Training and Development, consultants Judith G. Lindenberger and Lois J. Zachary offer vital questions for firms to ask themselves prior to implementing a program, including the following.

» What are our business reasons for developing the program? It shouldn't be developed just because the concept is popular.
» What organizational support exists and what needs to be developed? To begin with, such programs demand senior management support. Ideally, they will support the program if it, in turn, supports the company's values and goals.
» What will be the criteria for success? As a rule of thumb, anything you do within your organization should have a purpose. Ideally, the goals for mentoring programs should be long-term – from making the organization a better place to work to increasing productivity.
» What needs to be involved in developing the program? For instance, who should be involved? How should the process work?

» Who is going to manage, coordinate and oversee the program? Ideally, you need one person to serve as point person and mentoring coordinator to evaluate progress.

» Who else needs to be consulted? What other information do you need? Here's when you might want to study the practices of other successful mentoring programs.

» What mentoring already exists? You want to build a program that supports the informal mentoring relationships that are already going on.

» How will you communicate to employees information about the program? Ideally, you should develop a marketing plan just as you would create a plan if you were launching a new product into the marketplace.

» How quickly do you want to roll out the program? Is this a program that needs time to develop? Forcing participation by everyone can kill the program.

» How will you pair mentors and protégés? The examples above suggest some ways that companies facilitate partnerships. Ideally, you don't want shot-gun relationships.

» Why should a mentor say no? It is essential that participation be voluntary. People who choose not to participate in a mentoring relationship may feel that they don't have the time, that they can't provide the instruction a protégé wants, or that a protégé has chosen the mentor for the wrong reasons. Voluntary participation has been found to contribute more to the program's success. You don't want to enlist mentors who won't accept the commitment required to be a mentor.

» Are there pairings you should avoid? You want to pair protégés with mentors who can and want to help them reach their learning goals. It doesn't hurt if there is good chemistry between the pair, either. You don't want to develop a program that is limited to certain employees simply because they have been tagged as high potentials.

» What ongoing support should be made available to mentoring partners? Ideally, you need to have a mentoring coordinator, and that person should be available for advice and counsel.

» How often should mentoring partners meet? Ideally, the pair should have one meeting outside the office during their mentoring partnership – maybe on a sales call or watching a presentation or attendance at a trade conference. Beyond these special meetings, once a month face to face, via e-mail, or on the telephone should be sufficient.

» How many mentors should you encourage employees to have? While mentors shouldn't commit to more than two protégés, a mentee can actually build his or her own network of mentors to help in various areas.

As companies have jumped on the bandwagon in implementing formal programs, there has been concern raised about programs that force pairing. Tom Brown, writing in *Industry Week*,[1] raised the question whether forced pairings violated the spirit of mentoring. In their study of formal and informal mentoring relationships in *Personnel Psychology* (Autumn 1992), three researchers (G.T. Chao, P.M. Waltz, and P.D. Gardner)[2] compared formal and informal mentoring relationships on three outcome measures: organizational socialization, job satisfaction, and salary. The results found protégés in informal mentorships reported more career-related support from their mentors and higher salaries than protégés in formal mentorships. On the other hand, given the benefit that research has discovered from mentoring relationships – increased job satisfaction, employee retention, career advancement – and the likelihood that many relationships might not happen without such formal structures, then formal programs may make considerable dollars and sense to those firms with the resources to support the relationships.

NOTES

1 Brown, T.L. "Match up with a Mentor." *Industry Week*, **239** (1 October 1990), 18.
2 Chao, G.T., Waltz, P.M. & Gardner, P.D. (1992) "Formal and Informal Mentorships: A Comparison on Mentoring Functions and Contrast with Nonmentored Counterparts." *Personnel Psychology*, **45** (Autumn 1992), 619–36.

In Practice

Read in this chapter about coaching and mentoring programs at:

- » Sara Lee;
- » General Electric;
- » Johnson & Johnson;
- » Royal Dutch Shell;
- » The World Bank;
- » Saturn; and
- » Winthrop Pharmaceuticals.

As organizations have recognized the worth of training – skill training as in coaching and career training via mentoring – more and more companies have set up coaching and mentoring programs. In this chapter, we will describe some corporate coaching and mentoring initiatives, including those at:

» Sara Lee;
» AT&T;
» General Electric;
» NCR;
» Winthrop Pharmaceuticals;
» the World Bank; and
» Saturn.

Any discussion of corporate mentoring and coaching programs should be preceded, however, by a discussion of a broader application of mentoring and coaching throughout the world. I am referring to its application in worldwide programs like The Big Brothers, Big Sisters Program and The Grandparents Project in which adults serve as advisers and friends to young people. Narrowing it to the business community, coaching and mentoring are used for continuing professional development, as in the case of the Group Mentoring Program at the Australian Library and Information Association (ALIA). Typical of many programs that are designed to facilitate the transition of new graduates into the workforce, the ALIA program works with groups of new graduates to help their members develop and achieve their career plans. Some programs are like the ALIA in that they are organized by discipline whereas others are organized around gender or ethnicity.

Edison International sponsors the Job Skills Partnerships and Connected! mentoring programs that match at-risk high school students with mentors in the workforce. Connected! places students in management-mentored rotations, while JSP places students in union-mentored rotations. The program is held at multiple Edison locations and actively recruits other businesses to participate. Students often attend regular classes in the morning, and gain work experience in the field or in the office in the afternoon. Their participation builds technical skills but it also increases self-esteem and social skills and encourages the young people to remain in school. The employers who participate tap into a reliable source of qualified applicants that they can screen in advance for future entry-level spots.

When it comes to corporate programs, sometimes a specific problem prompted the organization's use of a program that was often labeled mentoring but frequently included skill coaching. For one, NCR had a shift in business focus – from selling product to selling solutions – and those veteran salespeople who found it difficult to sell invisible services as solutions to meet customer needs were mentored by salespeople who had successfully made the paradigm shift. The program's success led to its continuation as a means of helping new sales personnel get up to speed faster.

At Varian Associates Radiation Division, the problem was turnover. Costs spiraled as recent hires began to leave in large numbers due to the lack of promotional opportunity at this division of the US-based supplier of scientific instruments, vacuum technologies, and specialized contract electronic manufacturing services. Implementation of a mentoring program through an outside consultancy enabled veteran employees to share their practical know-how and old timers to learn about the latest software programs from their protégés, addressing the animosity that existed between the two groups. Staff turnover was reduced by 50 percent. Further, productivity increased. Prior to development of the mentoring program, the division had lost money for many years. It was even considered for the chopping block. But by the program's fifth year, the division had become a major profit center.

Sara Lee's Hosiery Division had a high percentage of female employees except at higher levels. The division chose a mentoring program in which female employees would be mentored to help them identify career path opportunities, including making a lateral move or contributing to an important project.

At Exxon's sales division, a structured mentoring program was instituted when it was found that informal mentoring was done by white male managers to white males. This led to a disproportionate staff turnover among women and minorities, who felt they had less growth opportunity than their white male counterparts. And, indeed, white males who had been mentored experienced improved performance and qualified for and earned promotions. Once women and minorities had the opportunity of mentoring, they reported feeling more valued. There was some concern expressed that mentors did not always give sufficient time to protégés, which prompted a change in responsibilities for mentors.

Mentoring has also been used to provide competency-based training at Scotiabank to overcome misconceptions about the bank business and unrealistic career expectations; to promote succession planning at Winthrop Pharmaceuticals to ensure replacements for top leaders, all expected to retire within four to five years; and to reduce staff turnover at AT&T's Consumer Products Lab, where valued employees who should have been mentored were unable to identify potential mentors and often quit as they realized that delayering within the organization left little opportunity for professional advancement. In the last case, group mentoring was used to match mentors with leading-edge expertise with small groups of high potentials who saw the advantage of acquiring intellectual capital from the mentors and the opportunity to participate in consumer product development projects on which mentors were working.

Andersen, the worldwide accountancy firm, believes that the time after a training program is every bit as important to partners as participation in its Partner Development Program. So Andersen provides post-work to reinforce learning. That post-work for new partners includes executive and peer coaching by established partners.

One of the most successful, long-lived companies in the world, Royal Dutch Shell/Shell International initiated its Leadership and Performance program (LEAP) to create leaders at every level throughout the organization. Among the skills that it regards as important to these up-and-coming leaders are coaching skills. Instead of individual managers acting as mentors, the organization relies on an internal resource for mentoring: its assessment centers. These help employees self-direct their careers in the same way that living managers might. They put employees in touch with the kind of learning experience or job assignment that will advance their careers.

Let's look more closely at some applications of coaching/mentoring initiatives.

THE RIGHT PLAYS ON THE JOB

Increasingly organizations are providing managers and even senior executives with coaches. Sometimes, the coaches are from within the organization. As you go higher within the organization, the likelihood of the coach being from outside the organization increases.

Experts estimate that there are 10,000 corporate coaches worldwide. According to a survey by Manchester Inc., an HR consulting firm located in Jacksonville, Florida, 59 percent of organizations currently offer coaching or other developmental counseling to their managers and executives.

GE Equity, a division of GE in Sandy Hook, Connecticut, is one of the companies that offer coaching to their senior executives. According to Stan Friedman, vice president of HR, the company implemented the program in 1997. At that time, the added support was provided only to those individuals at the senior level, those staffs reporting directly to the general manager. Since then, the company has rolled it out to managers.

Results vary. But among the better results was one senior person who was shocked by the 360-degree evaluation – it didn't match his perception of his performance. Based on the coaching, he became a better manager. "His team is much more respectful of him," according to Friedman.

The increase in coaching – internal and external – has a variety of causes.

» *Gap between senior executives and operational personnel due to downsizing of mid-ranks*. There is a need to create a new group of future leaders and/or prepare new hires for jobs they are not fully prepared to handle.

» *Demand by managers for opportunity to increase their employability by added support that coaching provides*. Today, everyone recognizes their need for constant development to keep pace. It's more of a competitive advantage to have one's own coach.

The Investment Management Group of Bank One in Glendale, Arizona, has had corporate coaches since 1999. Participants report greater job satisfaction, improved performance, and better ability to cope with difficult situations.

Another firm that uses coaches is CSX Transportation, Jacksonville, Florida. Coaches are used mainly to help high-potential employees and executives. "Lots of folks have blind spots around how their actions impact others," said Doug Kippel, CSX's director of organizational development. "They become myopic, focusing only on their own department's needs. Coaching extends their perspective."

THINKING ABOUT USING COACHES OTHER THAN SUPERVISORS?

Here are some considerations if you decide to either hire individuals for the specific role of coach or plan to contract with consultants to act as coach.

» One internal coach is needed for every 20 to 30 managers.
» External coaches will be spending a half hour to an hour with each manager, two to four times a month. Most coaches work with a manager for a minimum of three months, with the average relationship lasting six to nine months. Be sure to calculate the cost before considering a professional coach versus training managers in coaching skills.
» Comparing internal and external coaches, internal coaches know the systems, organizational culture, and how success is measured. Relationships can be long-term if need be. Since internal coaches are often at lower levels than the senior executives they might be asked to coach, senior executives prefer outside consultants as coaches.
» Topics for coaching vary, but most frequently the issues are time management and career advancement. Most managers are asked to undergo a 360-degree feedback evaluation prior to coaching.

REVERSE MENTORING

The program at General Electric is called "Reverse Mentoring" but it might more appropriately be called "Reverse Coaching" in that senior executives are *coached on a skill*: technology. The idea for the senior management technology training program came from CEO Jack Welch, who recognized that most executives were overwhelmed by the new technology. So he instituted the program whereby about 1000 GE executives, including Welch, would spend time learning basic Internet skills and trends from Internet or technology experts from within the company.

What is the curriculum? Beginner topics include use of the search engines and Web-based e-mail (hotmail and mail.com) and multimedia; intermediate topics include online B2C shopping, use of chat rooms and instant messaging, and Web page design and hosting. The advanced topics include business commerce and business chat rooms, new business models, updates on wireless services, and application service providers.

IS REVERSE MENTORING FOR YOU?

Before you implement a program like that at GE, think carefully.

» *Ensure that executives recognize they have a problem*. You can't get senior executives to commit to mentoring from employees lower in the organization unless they accept their shortcomings.
» *Identify experts in the field*. In GE's case it was technology-knowledgeable employees. The organization partnered one expert with one senior manager and scheduled regular meetings to see that training took place.
» *Teach experts to teach*. When non-trainers teach others, they need some basic instruction on training. At the very least, they need to start with the basics then move to more advanced topics. Additionally, they need to plan their sessions – particularly with busy senior executives – and have a destination or goal for each meeting.

THE DOLLAR SAVINGS FROM MENTORING AND COACHING

As important as training is, during today's tight economic times it is often one of the first expenditures that is cut. So in November 2000, when the semiconductor industry began to soften and budgets were cut, Larry Raskin, director of training and development at ADI, focused attention away from costly conferences, business school classes, and vendor-delivered classroom and Web-based training. Instead, he launched a formal companywide program that linked executives with up-and-coming employees. Raskin said, "Good coaching and mentoring programs are recession-proof."

ADI has always had informal mentoring. Under the structured program, however, mentors and protégés go through a day-long program, half of which is spent learning about being a mentor or protégé. The other half of the day is spent, after being paired, planning the new relationship.

RECESSION-PROOF COACHING AND MENTORING

» *Communicate the benefits of the program*. At Analog Devices, there was a lot of excitement and enthusiasm for the program among senior managers and younger employees when it was announced.
» *Clarify roles*. It isn't enough to teach mentors their responsibilities. Protégés, too, need to know what they are expected to do to get full benefit from the partnership.
» *Plan the new relationship*. Each pair of mentors and protégés need to have time to discuss how they will work together. Analog Devices included a half time in their full-day training program for such discussion and decision making. Whether the relationship is formalized or not, such discussion should take place. If the program is formalized, the company may want to nurture the pairing but it should not force fit individuals together or set up the ground rules for the new relationship. That should be up to the participants.

COACHING AND MENTORING AS PART OF LEADERSHIP DEVELOPMENT

Organizations have come to recognize that developing future leaders is not a luxury. Rather, it is a strategic necessity. Forward-thinking organizations have initiated leadership development programs in which coaching and mentoring play an important part. Among these companies are Johnson & Johnson, the World Bank, and Saturn.

Johnson & Johnson

J&J's senior management sees the company's need for more and more leaders as critical to its growth. So the company has made a major commitment to executive development. The organization has three major corporate programs for leadership development: the Executive Conference, for senior executives and management board members, that is primarily an action learning experience in which real business issues are brought to the leaders for collaborative problem solving and innovation; the Executive Development Program that is a three-week course for high-achieving managers considered to have the potential to move up to the senior management ranks, in which participants focus on leadership, teamwork, and change through business-issue, specific, action learning; and the Leadership Challenge, which communicates J&J's standards for leadership to directors and other new leaders at its various locations worldwide via group training.

What about coaching and mentoring? Corporate research has determined that among the practices that can affect career success for employees are mentoring, coaching, and feedback.

So the Executive Conference and Executive Development Program participants receive coaching on their action plans. J&J also offers coaching based on a participant's 360-degree feedback. In the Leadership Challenge, a faculty member from Corporate Education and Development (CED) offers leadership, coaching, and teamwork advice to the teams. There are around 190 J&J companies (of which more than 130 are outside the US), and mentoring initiatives vary. Some operating companies have formal programs, while others believe that mentoring should be strictly voluntary. Centrally, J&J has its "standards of leadership" on its intranet and these are accompanied by a coaching section for each one of the five standards. The five leadership standards are a reflection of strategic mission:

» customer/marketplace focus to create value for customers;
» innovativeness to spur business growth;

» willingness to build interdependent partnerships;
» positive attitude toward change and ability to manage complexity; and
» creation of an achievement environment where people can provide optimal performance.

The World Bank

The World Bank started its first mentoring initiative for women in Asia in 1997. Since then, it has begun 16 mentoring programs under one umbrella, each demand-driven. The company keeps a database of employees who have agreed to act as mentors.

Some programs are region-specific, such as the Africa or Asia mentoring groups. Some are topic-specific, such as the legal or transportation efforts mentoring groups. Each program has its own coordinator, and these coordinators – all of whom have full-time jobs in the bank – meet every two months to discuss progress success. Coordinators are expected to have good interpersonal skills and not only a commitment to the mentoring effort but also to the bank itself – they must be planning on staying with the bank for the next five years. Mentors are allowed two mentees.

Each mentoring group has its own steering committee of six to eight employees who plan social gatherings and match mentors to employees and otherwise oversee the program activities. Training is provided for both mentors and mentees. In pairing mentors and protégés, the mentoring committees check to see that no reporting relationship exists and that there is at least one grade level that separates mentors from mentees. An effort is made to match cultural similarities and educational levels, like pairing a PhD to an employee with a doctorate.

The process at the bank is called "facilitated mentoring," but there are no guidelines regarding the number of sessions over time. The intent of meetings is not to set an action plan to achieve a specific goal, but rather to offer feedback.

After two months, mentoring partners are asked if they are meeting and how the mentoring process is working. Protégés are not asked if they like or dislike their mentors. There is not only oral feedback but also a written evaluation that allows each partner to rate the pair's progress in career planning, discussion of organizational culture, and refinement of interpersonal skills. A third evaluation is used to get feedback from the pair on the mentorship level achieved. The World Bank also uses an outside consultancy to do a final evaluation, to determine the return from the partnership.

Mentors have said that they have become better listeners, demonstrate greater interest in coaching staff, and believe that the experience was useful. Mentees report that the mentoring relationship has raised their morale, increased their capabilities, and contributed to shared learning. Most report that the mentorship process included career guidance and advice.

Saturn

The car company Saturn encourages informal mentoring throughout the organization. The human resources department identifies team members who have been successful in different aspects of work, such as balancing work/family issues, leading teams, and managing disputes, and then points people with similar problems to these people.

The company also supports African-American and Hispanic men's and women's groups that have come together informally and naturally for the purpose of mentoring.

But Saturn does much more. Every Saturn team member has an individual training profile and a personal goal of attending 92 hours of training annually. To track employees' training progress, Saturn has a central Education Tracking system (ET), a mainframe computer system offering worldwide access to more than 1900 users. It houses all employees' individual training plans and progress toward their annual goals. The system also contains course abstracts, class schedules, and instructor information, and it is accessible to every training-point person on every team throughout Saturn, including car builders on the plant floor.

In charge of the development of self-managed teams, as well as their day-to-day production initiatives, are Operations Module Advisors (OMAs). The first level of partnered leadership, OMAs come in pairs (one OMA is union, the other management) and are responsible for a module (10 teams) with a crew of 100 members. This setup lends itself naturally to mentoring and coaching relationships. A new management OMA can be paired with an experienced union OMA on the job to make the transition easier and foster knowledge sharing. HRM at Saturn looks for good fits by using such tests as the Meyers-Briggs personality inventory.

As far as coaching is concerned, it is a requirement of all leaders at Saturn, and is considered essential training for all of them. Indeed, their fulfillment of their responsibility as coach is very much a part of each leader's performance evaluation.

THE ROLE OF COACHING AND MENTORING IN LEADERSHIP DEVELOPMENT

» *Coaching and mentoring do not have to be structured to work*. People with the willingness to create future leaders often accept responsibility for developing the potential of younger managers without a formal program.

» *Management must support the concept*. While the programs need not be formalized, it must be clear to all that management believes in the benefits of coaching and mentoring for such pairing to occur.

» *Formal pairing should be supported with consideration of fit*. Whether fit is measured statistically with a personality test or simply by meeting with likely partners before the pairing, fit is critical to the success of either a coaching or mentoring relationship.

» *Work between partners must have purpose*. Playing at management doesn't build the leaders that companies want. Real problems that can be addressed by coach and coached or mentor and protégé create the opportunity for success which can truly cement the relationship.

PEER MENTORING TO SUPPORT NEW PERSONNEL

Remember when you were a new employee? You weren't sure exactly what to do or how to do your job. Everything was new. But you wanted to be successful, which you knew meant that you had to be seen as a contributing, creative, responsible employee.

But you aren't the only one who wants you to be successful. Yes, your organization wants the work relationship to succeed. After all, if it doesn't, it will have to pay to recruit a replacement for you. But your new peers are equally interested in your success. If you don't carry your weight, guess who will have to do so? Your co-workers, that's who. Which explains why employees at the Ohio State University Extension have set up a peer mentoring program with the support of the 88-county University Extension organization.

The program begins with a form that each potential mentor and protégé are both asked to complete. The bio-sketch form includes information about background, experience, work-related interests, specialization, hobbies, non-work interests, and so forth. After 3 months and then 12 months, evaluations are conducted to assess satisfaction with the pairing and the process. Since mentor and protégé may be located several counties apart, problems may have arisen because of locations of both parties. Maybe it is simply the problem of time commitment.

Pairs are expected to meet six or more times over a 12-month period. A special feature of the program is the establishment of a district mentoring contact. A district is defined as an administrative group of 6 to 19 extension units, and a contact in each district helps to locally facilitate and monitor the progress of each mentor/protégé pair. Contacts are responsible for maintaining communication with the pairs, following up with protégés two weeks and three months after pairing, and serving on the State University mentoring developmental committee.

Since the peer mentoring program was formed in 1997, 100 mentor/protégé partnerships have been formed. Although the program was designed to provide support for new employees during their first year, the pairings have continued beyond that point. For the experienced mentor, the program enables them to perfect their coaching skills. For new staff, the experience offers temporary support until they become more familiar with other co-workers and find links to others within the organization, sometimes to personally chosen mentors within the organization.

Think a little about this program. To a great extent this is a self-instituted "buddy program." The term is one most frequently used to refer to an employee selected by a manager to orient a new employee to his or her job. But the success of the Ohio program suggests that there is no reason why employees can't be encouraged to use the same tool to help new colleagues settle in. It is an effective way to assist in cultural integration and orientation, as well as skill training.

PEER MENTORING PLUSES

Peer mentoring programs like that at Ohio State University Extension are special in two respects.

» *They are formed by the employees themselves*. Employees demonstrate a commitment to the organization's success by their willingness to help new hires succeed in their jobs.
» *They are supported by management*. District contacts ensure that pairings are working out. If they don't, they can recommend other relationships for both parties, ones that are productive for both individuals.

The benefits should be self-evident:

» employees are available to answer day-to-day operational issues;
» new hires will feel more at home with the organization in a shorter period of time;
» the initial confusion and uncertainty faced by all new hires is lessened;
» manager/supervisor time with new employees is freed up to deal with other issues;
» the new hire is able to add value to the workforce more quickly, leading to increased self-confidence; and
» the buddy feels more involved and committed to the organization's goals.

Some individuals might question these relationships as mentor-like. After all, peers are not going to be held responsible for the new hire's professional advancement. And mentors are typically more experienced. But peers can satisfy two critical roles of a mentor: role model and coach.

MORE THAN GOOD FEELINGS

Yes, mentoring can generate good feelings, but it also yields bottom-line results. At DLR Group, a 600-person architectural/engineering firm with regional offices in Omaha, Seattle, Minneapolis, and Phoenix, mentoring has contributed to the following:

» transmission of useful knowledge;
» more fluid project delivery;
» improved communication;
» guidance to staff; and
» greater accountability.

Uncertain whether a mentoring program would work, the organization began with a beta program, setting up mentoring relationships both across disciplines and up and down the firm's hierarchy. Those who served as mentors were expected to handle their new role during the normal course of project delivery. Mentors and protégés were selected according to each protégé's perceived need. Mentors were expected to offer hands-on assistance, not sit back like a guru and offer words of wisdom.

Mentoring opportunities would not be artificially created. Rather, when they arose, they would be utilized by the mentor. For instance, when a protégé traveled with a mentor to a client meeting, the mentor used the occasion to review the agenda and work with the protégé to design how the upcoming meeting would be managed. In another instance, a protégé being groomed for role of project manager was able to query his project architect mentor on the project's status.

Reverse mentoring also was utilized. In one instance, a junior expert in CAD mentored a senior project manager who wanted, but lacked, CAD skills.

The initiative went through three stages: training, during which the mentor tutored the protégé; coaching, in which the mentor provided constructive feedback, and finally, more traditional mentoring, in which the mentor offered more general advice.

The beta test focused on key aspects of project management, from subjects like speaking and effective listening to team building and client management. In terms of administrative skills, mentoring covered budgeting, negotiations, risk management, and meeting management, among other subjects.

The beta test was so successful that the decision was made to implement the program in three disciplines covered in the firm's Phoenix office – education, criminal justice, and private sector commercial construction.

MENTORING MAKES GOOD BUSINESS SENSE

Mentoring isn't worth the time or money unless it yields real worth to the organization. Without that reality, it is hard to persuade managers to give the time to up-and-comers. Some key points at DLR Group are worth remembering.

» The program began with a beta test to build support. A case of "small wins can generate interest."
» The mentoring process didn't require senior managers to mentor junior staff; indeed, just the opposite took place where the need existed.
» The program did not ask mentors to take time away from their day-to-day responsibilities to pontificate. Rather, the process was very hands-on, with time found whenever possible to coach the protégé.
» The tasks for which mentoring would be provided were specified and were very particular to the mission of the organization – like project management and client management.

WANTED: IT TALENT

We've described how mentoring has been used with new hires. But let's look at its application when there is a shortage of applicants and consequently a retention issue. I'm talking about how mentoring is being used by high-tech firms like Lucent and Hewlett-Packard. There has been renewed interest in mentoring and high-tech organizations have been at the forefront of this revival in interest due to the shortage of IT talent and their desperate need to retain the talent they have.

According to Gail Holmes, CEO of Mentium Corporation in Minneapolis, a designer and executor of mentoring programs, "IT talent, in particular, is in such high demand that an organization can't afford to lose these employees to a competitor. Mentoring translates into long-term viability, profitability, and shareholder value because that organization won't have to constantly replenish its staff."

Lucent Technology sees its Information Technology Leadership Development Program as critical to identifying and developing its talented IT professionals. And a key element of the program is a mentoring initiative. Protégés are matched with senior mentors for a one-year relationship in which the mentor provides care or guidance. The program attracts network engineers, technical managers, and middleware developers, as well as non-technical support staff.

The mentoring experience allows the IT employees to learn from their mentors' experiences, to be more visible within the organization, to network, and to learn about trends and resources within the company. The program also helps new hires to be assimilated more quickly into the organization. At many organizations, it falls on the shoulders of the new hires to guide themselves through the organization maze and ultimately find their own mentors, which is difficult even in small organizations but can be progressively more difficult the larger the firm. Having a formal program makes such a process much easier for new hires but it also sends a clear message from Day One to IT recruits that the company cares for their successful orientation into the organization.

The mentors at Lucent also welcome the opportunity since it gives them insights into the organization beyond their department boundaries. Not only do they get insights about other business units in the company, but they also learn how to be better communicators and become recognized as leaders.

Hewlett-Packard believes that its mentoring program has provided savings in recruitment costs. Its eight-year-old Accelerated Development Program is a year-long program that includes development planning, mentoring, leadership workshops, and external education. Its purpose is to groom both IT and non-IT middle managers. Hewlett-Packard spends about $30,000 to $35,000 on each person who goes through the program, and it has enrolled at least 100 employees annually.

At IBM, an initiative called the IBM Executive Resource Program has been especially helpful to women working in IT, a male-dominated discipline for the most part. The company believes that women need positive role models in leadership positions. Under-represented as they are in IT, and also unsure of the opportunities available to them in IT, they need to believe that the company is supportive of their career advancement. Which is the role of the mentoring initiative.

IBM has also created the Women of Color and Women in Technology subcommittees, the Mentoring and Employee Development Program, and the Global Women's Leadership conference, which encourage women to network and form mentoring relationships.

FINDING A PURPOSE FOR MENTORING

Mentoring is designed to help top talent advance in their careers. Some talented individuals within your organization need such support more than others. Within your management team, consider the following.

» *Mentoring by disciplines*. Would a mentoring program for those in hard-to-fill positions support employee retention efforts as well as contribute to a solid leadership team?

» *Mentoring by gender*. If you believe that women managers have a tough time making it to the top rungs of your organization, you may want to consider gender-related mentoring.

» *Diversity mentoring*. Are white males the only people within your organization with access to mentors? Does your organization have a disproportionate number of white senior managers? If so, you may want to set up programs that offer value-added coaching to members of minority groups to provide them with the same opportunity for mentoring as others within your organization.

Key Concepts and Thinkers

A glossary of coaching and mentoring terms, from A to Z.

Here's a glossary from A to Z on coaching and mentoring.

Active listening - In the context of coaching and mentoring, active listening means listening to what the other person is saying without interruptions and accepting what he or she is saying as genuine, at least to him or her, and not injecting one's own views, opinions, or solutions.

Aggressive communication - Blunt, demanding communication expecting compliance.

Assertiveness - Communication in a positive, sincere, confident manner that demonstrates respect for others.

Blanchard, Kenneth - Blanchard's book *The One-Minute Manager*, written with Spencer Johnson,[1] was much ridiculed by academics when it was first published in 1982. But since then it has sold over 7 million copies and has been translated into over 25 languages. That book, and later ones as well, point to the role that managers can play in inspiring winners - in essence, assuming the role of coach.

Buddy system - An alternative to mentoring in which new hires are put under the wing of someone experienced in the job.

Burns, James MacGregor - A political scientist, Burns wrote *Leadership*[2] in which he identified two forms of leadership - transformational and transactional leadership - that reflect on the purpose of coaching and mentoring. Transformational leadership "occurs when one or more persons engage with others in such a way that leaders and followers raise one another to higher levels of motivation and morality. Their purposes, which might have started out separate but related ... become fused." Think coaching or mentoring. As to transformational leadership, it is concerned with engaging the hearts and minds of others. Again, think coaching or mentoring. Burns wrote that transformational leadership required a number of skills, including the ability to coach and develop others.

Career development plans - Agreements between manager and employee that spell out exactly what formal support (time off, travel, expenses, and so on) they will receive to develop their skills and when they will receive it. Career development plans contain milestones for the achievement of learning goals and descriptions of any other resources and support needed to meet the goals that you agree on.

Chain of command – This reflects the hierarchical structure within organizations – the many levels of position within the non-managerial ranks and through the management ranks.

Coach – Someone, usually a manager, who meets regularly with another, usually an employee, and provides feedback to motivate and alert to potential problems.

Coaching – A framework for continuous performance improvement in which one individual provides regular feedback to another about his or her job- or work-related performance.

Collaboration – Cooperation and willing assistance in some kind of effort.

Constructive criticism – A misnomer, since criticism is by nature negative. Feedback should focus on how job performance can be improved.

Counseling – One-on-one interviews in which negative performance is the subject of the discussion. The intend is to turn around the performance and, if not, terminate the employee.

Critical incident technique – An approach to appraisal, it is a collection of recorded anecdotes about good and poor work and behavior. In CIT measurement of performance, the manager records incidents of significant work activities of both a positive and negative nature and uses these as part of coaching or mentoring sessions.

Cross-gender mentoring – An individual of one gender mentors someone of another gender. Now on the increase, cross-gender mentoring was rare in the past due to likelihood of charges of sexual harassment, gossip and speculation about the relationship between the individuals of different genders, and the like. However, companies have come to recognize how cross-gender mentoring can eliminate stereotypical thinking.

Delegation – The act of entrusting others with assignments and responsibilities. In terms of delegation, the coach's goal is to be able to delegate as much as possible, very different from the doer, who prefers to do the work himself or herself.

Diversity management – Differences in economic class, religious background, regional allegiance, and family structure and traditions are acknowledged and respected. In the context of mentoring, cross-cultural mentoring occurs when someone from one or more than one ethnic group mentors one or others from a different ethnic group.

Doer - In the context of coaching/mentoring, a doer's activity is the reverse of coaching/mentoring in that the focus is on the task issues of the work and/or the group's performance rather than on maximizing the talents and abilities of employees to their fullest to achieve high level of productivity (the coaching approach).

Drucker, Peter - In *The Practice of Management*[3] and *Management: Tasks, Responsibilities and Practice*,[4] Drucker identifies five roles for managers: to set objectives; to organize; to motivate and communicate; to measure; and, relevant to this book, to develop people. Drucker wrote, ''The function which distinguishes the manager above all other is this educational one.'' In Drucker's view, a major contribution of managers is giving others the ability to perform. Indeed, he believed that this role was one of five in which practices were required to ensure a positive work climate and culture; that is, there must be high performance requirements, no condoning of poor or mediocre performance; and rewards must be based on performance.

Employee compliance - Employees do as they are told, and work gets done, but the motivation is usually outside - based on fear - rather than from self-motivation.

Empowerment - Freedom given others to get work done as they see fit; should not be granted without pre-training to qualify the individual to make effective/efficient decisions.

Expectations - Standards set or goals/objectives, agreed between coach/mentor and coached and mentee or protégé.

Facilitation - As defined by *Merriam Webster's Collegiate Dictionary*, it is ''the act of making something easier.'' In the context of coaching, it refers to the need to listen as the employee speaks, to ask hypothetical questions to get him or her to think about the consequences of the actions he or she plans, and so forth. In the context of teams, it would include efforts to encourage discussion, including resolving conflicts among participants.

Feedback - Information communicated to an individual or team about job-related performance or behavior. The goal of feedback is to let employees know whether they are, or are not, making progress toward an agreed-on target or standard or behaving in a manner to support career aspirations.

Forming, storming, norming, performing – The four stages of team development, from identification of team members (forming), to decision about the mission and tasks for each (storming), to pursuit of tasks (norming), to completion of the team mission (performing).

Goal setting – Defining what needs to be accomplished in performance to achieve desired results. During coaching or mentoring, it refers to the process by which objectives are agreed on by coach and coached or mentor and mentee.

Learning organization – A continually adapting organization in which workers are empowered to expand their competencies, to identify and solve problems, and to find and build on opportunities.

Listening for feelings – In coaching/mentoring communications, the feelings often are more important than the facts, and coaches/mentors need to put aside words to get a sense of feelings conveyed.

Management by objectives (MBO) – One of several appraisal programs, most popular around the 1970s and 1980s, in which accomplishment of objectives set by manager and employee were used to evaluate employee performance over 12 months.

Management by phoning around (MBPA) – Similar to MBWA (see below) but done via phone, in which behavior is observed, and communication is maintained, with employees offsite (telecommuters, field sales personnel).

Management by walking around (MBWA) – A method of management to ensure that managers are visible to employees and able to maintain one-on-one communications. In the process, a manager can observe employee behaviors that can be the subject of subsequent coaching/mentoring sessions.

Maslow, Abraham – This behavioral scientist is best known for his "hierarchy of needs" – a concept he first published in 1943. Maslow argued that there was an ascending order of needs that had to be understood for people to be motivated. First, there are the physiological needs of warmth, shelter, and food. Once these basic needs are met, others emerge to dominate. Next come the safety needs, then social or love needs, and then ego or self-esteem needs. Ultimately, with each need satisfied comes what

Maslow labeled "self-actualization," as the individual achieves his or her own personal potential. Maslow's work is relevant to the subject of coaching/mentoring in that it suggests techniques to enable employees/managers to achieve self-actualization. It makes this pinnacle in his hierarchy dependent on feedback.

McGregor, Douglas – In his book *The Human Side of Enterprise*,[5] McGregor introduced the concepts of Theory X and Theory Y. X was traditional carrot-and-stick thinking built around the assumption that people were all inherently lazy, needing to be supervised and motivated, regarding work as a necessary evil to provide money. Theory Y, on the other hand, was based on the principle that people want and need to work, and the role of organizations is to liberate people's abilities to maximize their contribution to the organization. In that McGregor argues that the average person learns, under the right conditions, not only to accept but to seek responsibility, he seems to support the worth of coaching and mentoring. But even more significant were McGregor's four kinds of learning relevant for managers: intellectual knowledge; manual skills; problem solving skills; and social interaction. The last points to the worth of feedback in social settings. He pointed out that since we get little feedback of real value related to the impact of our behavior on others, such problematic behavior continues, which makes it easy to blame us for our stupidity or bad habits in social settings. Instead, our mistakes are discussed by our colleagues when we are not present to learn, a situation that mentoring – even coaching – by a well-meaning supervisor could prevent.

Mentee – The individual – employee or manager – who is mentored.

Mentor – Someone who offers knowledge, insight, perspective, or wisdom that is especially useful to the other person.

Mentor programs – Mentor programs are formalized programs in which employees are assigned to more senior employees to assist the new employee in learning the rules and norms of the organization, help the employee to solve political and work-related problems, and orient the employee in career development.

Mentoring hubs – The traditional one-on-one relationship redefined to include a mentor working with a number of mentees.

Mintzberg, Henry – *The Nature of Managerial Work* by Mintzberg[6] identified various roles of managers, including the interpersonal role of leader, motivating employees very much like a sports coach. The interpersonal responsibilities of managers made up one of three categories of work roles for managers. The other two were informational and decisional roles. Interpersonal roles included figurehead, representing the organization to outsiders, and liaiser, maintaining lateral contacts. The informational roles included monitor of information flows, disseminator of information to employees, and spokesperson, communicating information to outsiders. The decisional role encompassed entrepreneur or designer of change, disturbance handler or handler of non-routine events, resource allocator or decider of who gets what and does what, and negotiator.

Mission – A goal or purpose; the term is usually used to describe the reason for an organization.

Outcome – Term for desired result or accomplishment, often used in referring to objectives in results-oriented appraisals.

Participative management – Involvement of employees in decisions made. Too often, participative management entails decisions made by management then communicated to employees for input that is never listened to. Popular concept in the 1970s.

Passive communication – Meek, hesitant, indirect, laissez-faire manner that renders coaching useless.

Pluggers – A term used to describe employees who perform to a standard but no more; while they demand little supervision, they also get little attention and consequently too often their full potential is not realized.

Positive reinforcement – Rewards – tangible and intangible – that encourage repetition of desired behavior; the opposite is negative reinforcement, in which no reward is given or punitive actions are taken to discourage repetition of nonproductive or counterproductive behavior.

Protégé – Another term for mentee, one who is mentored.

Situational management – A means of management in which the degree of management is based on the experience and self-confidence of the individual being supervised, coached, or mentored, and the nature and importance of the task involved.

Sponsor – That individual who has a team formed either for his or her own purpose or for the purpose of another individual or organization as a whole.

Stereotyping – Dismisses the individual differences that influence who a person is and ascribes a set of behaviors to everyone in a particular group based on personal background, physical appearance, and so forth.

Stretch – A term used in the context of coaching and appraisals that refers to the difference between previous performance or sameness in behavior and higher level of behavior.

Team coach – Leader or other individual who oversees the team, coaching participants, and the team as a whole to ensure clarity of mission, practice of ground rules to govern the team's operation, maintenance of administrative details, avoidance of conflicts and clear designation of assignments, and – most important – accomplishment of mission.

360-degree assessments – A performance management/employee development tool that gathers input on performance from a variety of individuals, including supervisors, employees, co-workers, and customers, to get an accurate assessment of behaviors.

Values – Beliefs or ideas by which the organization operates, for they are deemed critical to competitive advantage.

NOTES

1 Blanchard, K. & Johnson, S. (1982) *The One-Minute Manager*. William Morrow & Co., New York.
2 Burns, J.M. (1978) *Leadership*. Harper, New York.
3 Drucker, P. (1954) *The Practice of Management*. Harper & Row, New York.
4 Drucker, P. (1974) *Management: Tasks, Responsibilities and Practice*. Harper & Row, New York.
5 McGregor, D. (1960) *The Human Side of Enterprise*. McGraw-Hill, New York.
6 Mintzberg, H. (1973) *The Nature of Managerial Work*. Harper & Row, New York.

Resources

Articles, books, Websites, and organizations that can supplement your knowledge about coaching and mentoring.

ARTICLES

» "Mentoring," A White Paper by David B. Hutchins, Society for Human Resource Management, www.shrm.org/whitepapers/documents/default.asp?page_mentor1.asp.

Do successful people attract mentors or does mentoring create successful people? That's the dilemma the author attempts to answer. His conclusion is that a mentor can compensate for an individual's lack of experience, organizational connections, and influence during initial, mid, and later career years. In addition, such relationships can directly impact the workplace. Mentoring can be a catalyst to a learning organization, according to the author.

» "Reverse Mentoring" by the Info-Tech Research Group, HR.com.

Learn how Jack Welch of GE used reverse mentoring to teach 1000 GE executives about technology. The executives underwent "reverse mentoring," in which senior managers, including Welch, spent time learning from Internet and other technology experts from within the company. This learning included basic Internet skills, trends, and developments to which they had yet to become alerted, and protocol in chat rooms.

» "Mentoring as a Strategy" by Linda Saulnier, Career Resources, www.townonline.com/working/careerres/12159602.html.

This article points to the growing trend in which employers take a proactive approach to mentoring, pairing mentors and mentees. If the company thinks an employee has the potential to succeed, they select a mentor to give the individual an insider's view of the company, act as his or her confidant, and advise him or her on how to shed weaknesses and build upon strengths. Based on interviews with executives who have implemented formal mentor programs, the author concludes that mentoring increases productivity and demonstrates to employees that they are valued by their company. Their loyalty to the company increases, thereby reducing turnover. The author adds: "Mentoring is not on-the-job training; employees must master the basic job skills long before mentoring comes into the play. Nor is it a corrective process for substandard performance. Rather, it is a collaboration to expand knowledge to meet new challenges."

» "Mentoring Media," The Mentor Center, www.teachermentors.com/ MCenter%20Site/MentoringMedia.html.

Technology holds great promise for mentoring people in remote settings – from telementoring that uses e-mail and videoconferencing and other technologies to connect the mentor and protégé for conversations to mentoring software that replaces a paper-based professional portfolio, to how-to instruction videos and audio tapes.

» "Peer Mentoring to Support New Personnel" by Linda M. Kutilek and Cindy Taylor, www.wmich.edu/conferences/mentoring/personnel. html.

Use of peer mentoring ensures an early start for a new hire. The program at Ohio State University Extension Organization includes completion of a bio-sketch form that asks about background, experience, work-related interests, hobbies, and family. An evaluation is conducted after 3 to 12 months to assess satisfaction with the pairing and the process. Although often protégé and mentor are in separate districts, a mentor contact maintains communication with the pair to facilitate and monitor the progress of each mentor/protégé pair.

BOOKS

» Stone, F.M. (1999) *Coaching, Counseling & Mentoring: How to Choose & Use the Right Technique to Boost Employee Performance.* AMACOM, New York, NY.

This book clarifies the differences among coaching, counseling, and mentoring, noting that the techniques may be somewhat similar but the objectives are very different. The author shows how coaching will enable managers to "add stretch" to employees' performance, accurately assess development and training needs, and develop teams adept at problem solving and brainstorming, whereas mentoring enables managers to sustain their top performers' motivation despite limited rewards or opportunities for advancement, prevent new employees from picking up the bad habits of existing staff, and helps them possess the right corporate values. As far as counseling is concerned, Stone shows how counseling can build honest, open communications and turn around poor performance; if it doesn't work, she shows how proper documentation can protect in case of legal action by an aggrieved employee. The book shows not only how to practice each management technique correctly but also the pitfalls if they are done wrongly.

» Peddy, S. (1998) *The Art of Mentoring: Lead, Follow, and Get Out of the Way*. Bullion Books, Houston, TX.

As the demand for experience and knowledge increases, organizations are helplessly watching the exodus of some of their most highly regarded employees. Those who remain lack any guidance and encouragement from more experienced managers and employees. What is the solution? The mentoring process. Knowledge and skills are passed down through stories and learned by working closely with those who have proved themselves in that arena (leaders). Followership comes from adhering to the advice and counsel provided. Once a mentee has gained the maturity and judgment to make it on his or her own, then the mentee is prepared to lead himself or herself, even mentor others. The how-to information comes in the form of a story of an internal consultant – the author – sent to a small company to renew motivation in the five marketers there or recommend their termination.

» Hargrove, R. (1999) *Masterful Coaching: Grow Your Business, Multiply Your Profits, Win the Talent* War. Jossey-Bass/Pfeiffer, San Francisco, CA.

This book acknowledges the importance of coaching for managers, supervisors, and HR professionals in every field. Based on Hargrove's six-step model of "transformational coaching," the book shows managers how to encourage employees to think and work better together, and thereby produce great results. Hargrove makes the advice special by including interviews with business, sports, and other leaders, who share their tips about coaching.

» Lacey, K. (1999) *Making Mentoring Happen*. Business & Professional Publishing Pty Limited, Sydney.

For those who want to institute a formal mentoring program within their organization – whether to reduce staff turnover, induct new employees more successfully, fast-track best employees, or make best use of their senior staff – this book outlines the concept and benefits for all those involved, then shows how a program can be implemented. Finally, the book gives training activities and sample documents to make the program run smoothly.

» Doyle, J.S. (1999) *The Business Coach: A Game Plan for the New Work Environment*. John Wiley & Sons, New York, NY.

Doyle takes the highly effective methods used by sports coaches and adapts them to business management scenarios. He offers practical advice on how supervisors can change their leadership skills to boost morale and increase productivity among "team" members. For one, he warns against the "quick fix" mentality and advises that coaching is a slow process if the coach is to build the open, trusting relationship that is the foundation of effective coaching. Included in the book are assessment guides, worksheets, and exercises.

» Johnson, H.E. (1997) *Mentoring for Exceptional Performance*. Griffin Publishing, Glendale, CA.

For those who want to institute formal mentoring programs, this book looks at how the technique can be used with teams and the organization culture as well as individuals. The author observes, "Thinking to implement a mentoring program is the first step in a series of important steps to strengthen your human resources. A systematic and thoughtful approach at the beginning will increase the likelihood of successful results."

» Gilley, J.W. & Boughton, N.W. (1995) *Start Coaching: How Performance Coaching Can Enhance Commitment and Improve Productivity*. McGraw-Hill Companies, New York, NY.

The book points out how coaching can build healthy and positive work relationships with employees and thereby increase motivation and performance. The author includes mentoring in his four phases of performance coaching and takes empowerment one step further, to employee self-esteeming. Finally, the author identifies 12 performance killers that can destroy all coaching initiatives, from judging to criticizing, to playing amateur psychiatrist, to labeling, to manipulative praising, to providing solutions, to advising, to ordering, to moralizing, to questioning, to threatening, to avoiding, to diverting, to arguing, to offering reassurances ("Don't worry about it; it will all work out OK").

» Cullen, J. & D'Innocenzo, L. (1999) *The Agile Manager's Guide to Coaching to Maximize Performance*. Velocity Press, Bristol, VT.

The authors make a strong point that managing is very different from coaching; managing has to do with the process of business, whereas coaching is about inspiring and empowering people. "Good managers who can coach their people make excellent leaders," according to the authors, who describe how a manager can adapt his or her coaching style to the employee, from top performers to inconsistent performers to mediocre performers to new hires with desire but a need to learn the job. The authors advocate that managers begin to coach from the first day they hire, that they practice the basic steps – delegate, support, direct, and coach (observe and recommend) – and remove obstacles in the way of employee achievement, and that they recognize that people will develop in varying degrees and ways – and can, upon occasion, fall back.

» Dotlich, D.L. & Cairo, P.C. (1999) *Action Coaching*. Jossey-Bass, San Francisco, CA.

Action coaching is different from other coaching in that the effort is linked to specific organizational issues. To use the authors' definition of action coaching, it is "a process that fosters self-awareness and that results in the motivation to change, as well as the guidance needed if change is to take place in ways that meet organizational needs." With action coaching, the goals for individuals are always determined in conjunction with the organization, an approach that has been proven by the authors in firms like Pfizer, Johnson & Johnson, Levi Strauss, Bank of America, Merck, and Arthur Andersen.

» Fournies, F.F. (2000) *Coaching for Improved Work Performance*. McGraw-Hill Companies, New York, NY.

The former professor at Columbia University's Graduate School of Business, Fournies examines specific problems that coaching identifies and offers advice on how to handle them and, better yet, what to do if the performance action plans don't work. Of especial interest is the chapter on "Coaching Analysis" that begins with an oft-neglected question – Does the employee know that a problem exists? – then moves on to address the following questions: Does the employee know what should be done? Does the employee know how to do it? Does the employee know why it should be done? Are there obstacles beyond the employee's control? Does the employee think that your way won't work? Does the employee think his/her way may be better? Does the employee think something else is more important? Are there positive consequences to the employee for performing appropriately? Does the employee recognize the negative consequences of inappropriately performing? Could the employee do it if he or she chose or are there personal problems creating a performance dilemma?

» Shea, G.F. (1994) *Mentoring: Helping Employees Reach Their Full Potential*. AMACOM, New York, NY.

Shea shows how mentoring has evolved from a career-focused methodology to become a technique to improve organizational or individual work performance. In relation to the latter quality, Shea says that mentoring "can be a tool for broadening the vision and capability of virtually every employee." The author points not only to the advantages for mentees and organizations in this new kind of mentoring but also to the benefits for mentors.

» Deeprose, D. (1995) *Team Coach*. AMACOM, New York, NY.

While many books incorporate team issues, this book is devoted entirely to the role of team leader as coach, including his or her role in facilitating communication among members, conducting long-term planning, supporting the career development of team members, resolving conflicts among participants, and measuring performance, even instituting team-based compensation programs.

» Hudson, F.M. (1999) *The Handbook of Coaching*. Jossey-Bass, San Francisco, CA.

If you are looking for a comprehensive resource guide on coaching that looks beyond business issues, this may be it. The book examines coaching for the living and the dying, for students and teachers, for managers and business leaders. Most important, throughout you will find bibliographies of articles and books and research studies. Taking a tip from formal performance assessments, the book suggests a coaching agreement between coach and coached to ensure clarity in the relationship and goals set.

» Crane, T.G. (2001) *The Heart of Coaching*. FTA Press, San Diego, CA.

This book advocates transformational coaching, pointing to how the technique creates an egalitarian, mutually supportive relationship rather than merely supporting the traditional supervisor/subordinate relationship. If the book's discussion of the emotional quality is critical to this transition, then it takes a step in that direction, pointing to how emotionally intelligent coaches are more able to foster self-responsibility and collaboration in employees and groups of employees (think teams). In Crane's view, transformational coaching is leadership at its best, for it creates and sustains a feedback-rich organization that is a competitive advantage today. Certainly, the role of coach he advocates is critical to the practice of 360 degree assessment throughout an organization.

» Hendricks, W. (ed.) (1996) *Coaching, Mentoring and Managing*. National Press Publications, Franklin Lakes, NJ.

The thinking here is pretty logical: in this period of down-sizing, layoffs, buyouts, and mergers, managers and HR professionals are faced with the challenge of boosting employee morale, and mentoring and coaching are means of doing that. The book suggests that coaching doesn't come naturally but is a skill that can be developed, and the book contains techniques to help develop your coaching and mentoring talents. For the supervisor, there are hundreds of practical, focused tools to make a team more positive, more productive, and more effective. It contains real-world advice as well as management-changing exercises that have been used by managers and organizations in practicing coaching/mentoring efforts.

ORGANIZATIONS

» MentorNet: www.mentornet.net/

The Electronic Industrial Mentoring Network for Women in Engineering and Science pairs women who are studying engineering or science at one of the participating colleges or universities with professional scientists and engineers working in industry and helps them form e-based mentoring relationships.

» National Mentoring Association of Australia: www.mentoring-australia.com/

The objectives of Mentoring Australia are to create a communication network for mentoring programs to share ideas and resources, promote mentoring, benchmark the principles of good practice, develop strategic alliances, establish a clearing house for training and resources, and promote advocacy of mentoring relationships.

» The Mentoring Group/CCC: www.mentoringgroup.com/Archive. html

Here you can find general information on mentoring and mentee planning tools, and advice to help mentees with vision statements and development plans. The organization, located in Grass Valley, California, offers tips for mentors and mentees, worldwide training programs, research on mentoring relationships, and an assortment of best practices assembled from around the world.

» Governor's Mentoring Initiative: www.flmentoring.org/myflorida/ governorsoffice/mentoring/corp_honor_roll.html

Designed to improve the quality of life for Florida's students, the program involves the business community, from CEO on down, in mentoring a child. To make the statewise corporate honor roll, a CEO must mentor a child for at least one hour a week and also adopt a companywide policy that supports the same efforts among employees. Firms on the honor roll include AutoNation, Burger King, Darden Restaurants, Disney, Florida Power Corporation, Universal Studios Escape, McKinsey and Company, and IBM. It's a model that other states may want to emulate to better educate their future business leaders.

» Society for Human Resource Management: www.shrm.org/hrmagazine/articles/

You don't have to be a member of SHRM to access the many articles available at this membership organization's home site. In particular, check out the section of articles on how formal mentoring programs are being used to ensure that top minority talent have the opportunity to rise through the ranks of their organization.

Ten Ways to Make Things Happen

Find out in this chapter:

» when the coaching process begins;
» how to create a positive environment in which coaching and mentoring efforts can be productive;
» how to use coaching and mentoring to maximize employee performance; and
» what pitfalls to avoid.

To best appreciate how to make coaching or mentoring successful, let's look at the subjects from the perspective of one who undertakes them. Here you will learn:

» where coaching begins;
» how to create a positive environment where coaching and mentoring can prosper;
» how to use coaching and mentoring to maximize employee performance; and
» what pitfalls to avoid.

1. HIRE THE BEST

This pertains to the role of coach. You want to hire for your department individuals who would continually be in search of more knowledge and be eager to develop new skills, who won't accept the current way of doing things and may challenge existing practices if they believe they have a better way, who want to know the whys and wherefores of things and won't accept anything without explanation, and who are dissatisfied if they don't have challenges.

Don't just hire the best but see that those you hire are suitably oriented to their new workforce.

To begin with, talk about the individual's job responsibilities. Review your assessment during recruitment to identify gaps in skills, knowledge, and attitudes and discuss a training program – on-the-job or off site – to help fill the knowledge gaps.

On that first day after hire, meet, too, with new employees to discuss department and organization missions, strategies, and tactics. If you want to get the most from your employees, you need to let them know as much as possible about the bigger corporate picture. That includes information about the company's financial situation. Whether news is good or bad, knowing the situation is better than speculating.

Don't forget, either, to talk about corporate values. As a mentor, you don't want only to read the list of values or beliefs critical to the company's competitive advantage. You want to discuss with a mentee how these values might translate into behaviors that will increase visibility and employability, and maybe lead to advancement if an opportunity arises.

From the perspective of coaching, employees will be better able to understand and accept the feedback they receive if they understand their role in the bigger picture.

Neither the coaching nor mentoring meetings are one-time conversations. Ideally, coaching sessions should be given monthly to all employees. Mentoring sessions may be held more or less frequently depending on a mentee's need. You may choose to mentor only one individual or several talented employees within your organization.

2. CREATE THE RIGHT CLIMATE

Coaching and/or mentoring can only exist in a climate that contributes to a free and open exchange of ideas. Toward that, give feedback, not criticism. Don't offer praise from discomfort about leveling about performance. Rather, be assertive, citing specifics to demonstrate the validity of your remarks.

As you share your feedback, do so in a manner that communicates that the errors in performance are learning opportunities. Tell the coached or mentee, "Okay, this isn't working. What can we learn from its failure?" Silence is an effective means of encouraging employees to test their ideas out because they realize that their coach/mentor knows that not all efforts will be successful – that the wrong decision doesn't mean that they are a failure.

You want the individual you are coaching or mentoring to come away from the one-on-one session with his or her self-esteem intact. Which means that you want to focus on the behavior and not the person. Consequently, you might tell someone who has many good ideas, but who frequently interrupts others with ideas as well, that you appreciate his or her creativity but that continued interruptions will mean the loss of others' thinking. This way, the person you are coaching leaves feeling appreciated yet aware of a behavioral shortcoming.

Equally important, look for improvements as well as problems in performance during coaching or mentoring. Coaching is a continuous improvement process. Likewise, mentoring. Acknowledge the positive behavioral changes. Even small improvements should be recognized, since such feedback can stimulate the employee to work on greater changes.

3. ACT AS A ROLE MODEL

This rule is as applicable to those who act as coach as to those who act as mentor. Remember the axiom, "Do what I say, not what I do." As either a coach or a mentor, you don't want your staff members to snicker and attribute such a phrase to you. You have to remember that when you are visible to your employees, your staff will be watching you *and* emulating you. Be sure that what you do is also is what you would want those you coach or mentor to do.

Most important, keep your promises. In particular, be sure to keep your promise to maintain open and honest communications with those you coach or mentor – to provide them with the opportunity to reach their potential, the opportunity for empowerment, and recognition and reward for excellence and outstanding performance.

4. DON'T IGNORE TRAINING NEEDS

Don't let your own tough work schedule cause you to forget your obligation to your employees or protégés by not providing earlier identified or evident training needs. Sometimes training needs only become evident after a few weeks or months on the job, or a job changes as the technology or procedures or rules change. Whatever the reason, in your role as coach or mentor, you need to regularly look for discrepancies between optimum performance and actual performance. The difference between the two is the training that is needed.

As mentor, you also want to look beyond the skills your protégé currently needs to identify skills that will contribute to the individual's potential for advancement. If classroom training is out of the question due to limited funds, consider alternative means by which the individual can gain the same learning – from a computer-based program to a book. Even a home study program is worthy of consideration, since travel and hotel accommodations – the biggest expenses of attendance at a workshop or seminar – are unnecessary.

Assignment as assistant on a project can also provide a learning experience for someone with the ability to learn from example. If it isn't one of your assignments, see if you can broker such a position for your mentee, asking a colleague to take on your mentee to help him or her learn a new skill. Don't think your task is done then. Monitor progress to be sure that the relationship works out for both.

Consider, too, participation in a team where the individual can learn from others via job shadowing or being given "stretch assignments" by a fellow team member.

5. SET LEARNING AND CAREER GOALS

Your employee needs to know what you expect him or her to gain from the training. In turn, he or she should share his or her aspirations with you. You may want to put in writing your commitment to helping him or her reach that position. Which means promising only that which you can deliver. Is there such a position within your organization? If so, what would the employee need to do to be considered? If there is no such opportunity within your organization, what opportunities might be within the individual's grasp with time?

For mentors, you should discuss learning and career goals at the start of the relationship and periodically thereafter at set milestones. These milestones may be set by you and your protégé. One or other of you may also ask to meet to discuss progress if problems are occurring. For instance, the protégé may feel you aren't as available as he or she needs, or you may feel that the mentee is not listening to your advice or that he or she is becoming too dependent on your help and thereby not working hard enough to achieve his or her goals.

You may want to put the learning and career goals and your responsibilities and those of the mentee on paper and sign the document.

As a coach, a written agreement between you and your employees will demonstrate your desire to help them to succeed in their jobs. The agreement here should identify the learning goals and the means by which they will be achieved. Ideally, you should have such a document for each and every one of your employees, and reviews should be monthly. At the very least, you should review development goals at the same time as you review job performance, which could be every trimester or quarter.

You may want to use the year-end annual assessment to identify the learning goals for the next year, basing learning goals on gaps between results anticipated and results accomplished. Discussion of the gaps can identify learning needs and can be the focus of training over the next 12 months.

6. KEEP IN MIND THAT COACHING AND MENTORING ARE ABOUT PERFORMANCE

They are not solely about development. Further, their purpose is not to address problems in performance. That's the role of counseling, the goal of which is to advise a troubled or troublesome employee before termination becomes necessary. Both coaching and mentoring aim to sustain, if not increase, the quality of performance, as a result of continual communication and managerial support.

Employees need to know where they stand in the organization – what they are doing right and what they are doing wrong – and how they can improve that standing. That's why feedback from coach or mentor is so critical. The protégé or employee also needs to be able to tell their mentor or coach when they need help or assistance. And both individuals need this dialog in a timely manner, on an ongoing basis, before a small dilemma grows into a serious problem that impacts their reputation within the organization or impacts the work of others.

7. BE AVAILABLE WHEN NEEDED

If your protégé or employee needs to speak, you need to find the time for him or her, which may mean more than sitting across the desk from the individual. According to Michael Dell, "Management in business today is different combinations of face-to-face, ear-to-ear, and keyboard-to-keyboard." Phone and e-mail communication will make you more accessible to your employee or mentee and you have to be willing to use such virtual communication when more traditional one-on-one performance communication isn't possible.

Some individuals may have doubts, but those managers who have tried it have found that e-mail, in particular, makes it easier not only for them to discuss frankly an employee's performance but also for their employees to share their dreams, aspirations, and, yes, vulnerabilities with their boss or mentor. After all, isn't it true that there are people who have met one another, fallen in love, and ultimately married all through using the Internet?

8. ACKNOWLEDGE IMPROVEMENT

Acknowledging good performance doesn't have to mean big bucks to an employee. Recognition of an improvement in performance of an employee or a major accomplishment by a mentee can come in the form of praise and other positive reinforcements. Unless you acknowledge the achievement, no matter how small it may be, the improvement isn't likely to be permanent and the accomplishment isn't likely to be repeated. Nor are either likely to be followed by bigger improvements or accomplishments over time.

As a manager, your responsibilities include coaching. Indeed, coaching may represent a major part of your work. Consider the benefits – ongoing performance improvement – of spending 20 minutes at least every month with each and every one of your employees. A meeting with a mentor can take place over lunch in which you both glory in the accomplishment which is as much yours as your protégé's. Ignoring the event because you are too busy tells the protégé that his or her achievement means little to you, which can put a spanner in the relationship.

9. ADDRESS PERSONALITY CONFLICTS

Admittedly, it is easier for a mentor to cope with a personality conflict than for a coach. A mentor needs to end the relationship. The mentor may have entered into the relationship without fully knowing the person. After working closely in a mentoring relationship, the mentor has discovered that he or she just can't get along with the individual. The protégé may be a hard worker and very talented, but the mentor and protégé are always at odds. Time spent with this individual could more productively be spent with another, equally talented employee who would be more willing to listen to the mentor's feedback.

If such is the case, the mentor needs to let the protégé know. Suggest another mentor who might be more suitable for the individual.

What about an employee's manager? Unfortunately, where a personality conflict exists, the manager can't reassign a direct report – no matter how much he or she might wish to do so. Rather, the situation demands that the manager, in his or her role as coach, meet with the employee and explore the reasons for the conflict between the two. The two may ultimately have to agree to disagree, which includes agreement by the employee that he or she, no matter what the personal feelings, will comply with instructions from the manager. But the discussion may also unearth coaching traps that the manager is falling into.

For instance, many coaches wrongly assume that staff members know the department's mission or goals, or fail to keep them informed when changes are made in either, and consequently confusion reigns. When such a situation recurs, it can undermine motivation and lead to personal feelings about the individual in charge. Without information on department goals, or with what seems to them like continual shifts in direction, a member of staff can grow weary. Often a personality conflict may be due not to *real* differences but rather to lack of clarity about assignments.

Personality conflicts can also be caused by managerial impatience. Coaches can easily fall into this trap after having explained the same task for the tenth time, learning about a stupid mistake that will cause a project setback, or reading a simple memo that needs editing.

A coach who fails to exhibit patience in such circumstances sends a message to an employee that he or she "can't believe just how stupid the employee is." Over time, it can build a fence between the manager and employee. Patience, on the other hand, creates a bridge. Patient coaches tell their employees that they recognize that they are human beings and, as such, have human fallibility, but that that is no reason to quit. Rather, as human beings with the capability of developing and improving performance, employees understand their boss's patience as evidence that he or she believes that they can succeed in their work. So they should try again.

10. GIVE CONSTRUCTIVE FEEDBACK

The key word here may be "feedback." Often we hear the phrase "constructive criticism," but criticism by its very nature is negative. Where problems exist, the feedback should suggest the means by which performance could be improved, not be filled with adverbs that suggest that the person *always* does wrong or *never* will improve. Nor should judgments be made about the protégé's or coached person's attitude. Suggesting that someone is lazy or argumentative or uninterested in his or her work is demoralizing, and more likely to decrease the individual's level of performance than improve it. Besides, attitudinal feedback gives a coached person or protégé no direction to help him or her improve performance.

After all, that's the purpose of coaching and mentoring, isn't it?

Frequently Asked Questions (FAQs)

Q1: How can you improve your employees' skills and enhance their careers?

A: Answers can be found in Chapter 1.

Q2: Are coaching and mentoring different?

A: The answer is yes. Learn how they differ and why this is important in Chapter 2.

Q3: How have coaching and mentoring evolved since their beginnings in the Stone Age?

A: Find out in Chapter 3.

Q4: How has the technological revolution created both a need for coaching and mentoring and a means of facilitating their use?

A: See Chapter 4.

Q5: Why do coaching and mentoring facilitate global management?

A: Learn how in Chapter 5.

Q6: How do coaching and mentoring programs work?

A: Find out in Chapter 6.

Q7: Why initiate a coaching or mentoring program?

A: The reasons vary. Learn the many causes behind such programs in Chapter 7.

Q8: What is a "plugger?" Do you know what a "mentoring hub" is?

A: Look at the glossary, from A to Z, in Chapter 8.

Q9: Do you want to read more about coaching and mentoring?

A: If so, see Chapter 9.

Q10: What do you need to know to be successful at coaching or mentoring?

A: Look at Chapter 10.

Index